DEFINING
MOMENTS
IN JOURNALISM

Media Studies Series

DEFINING MOMENTS
IN JOURNALISM

NANCY J. WOODHULL
ROBERT W. SNYDER

EDITORS

TRANSACTION PUBLISHERS

NEW BRUNSWICK (U.S.A.) AND LONDON (U.K.)

Copyright © 1998 by Transaction Publishers, New Brunswick, New Jersey. Originally published as *Media Studies Journal,* Spring 1997. Copyright © 1997 by Media Studies Center and The Freedom Forum.

This book is printed on acid-free paper that meets the American National Standard for Permanence of Paper for Printed Library Materials.

Library of Congress Catalog Number: 98-5534
ISBN: 0-7658-0442-5
Printed in the United States of America

Library of Congress Cataloging-in-Publication Data

Defining moments in journalism / edited by Nancy J. Woodhull and
    Robert W. Snyder.
        p.   cm. — (Media studies series)
    "Originally published in the Media studies journal, Spring 1997"—
Verso t.p.
    Includes bibliographical references.
    ISBN 0-7658-0442-5 (alk. paper)
    1. Journalism—United States—History—20th century. I. Woodhull,
Nancy J. II. Snyder, Robert W., date. III. Media studies journal.
IV. Series.
PN4867.D36   1998
071'.3'0904—dc21   98-5534
                                                                CIP

This book is dedicated to Nancy J. Woodhull
Born Perth Amboy, N.J., March 1, 1945
Died Pittsford, N.Y., April 1, 1997

The greatest rewards always materialize from confronting uncertainty. We gain the most when we dare to be different.
—Nancy J. Woodhull,
Keuka College commencement address, May 26, 1996

Contents

As Edward R. Murrow and his protégés went to the airwaves in the early days of World War II, they transformed broadcasting, argue two authors. "The key, he told the members of his team, was to report for the ear, not the eye—or, to put it another way, to report for the *mind's* eye."

"When Gov. Orval Faubus suddenly deployed the Arkansas National Guard to prevent the invasion of Little Rock's Central High School by nine black children, I had spent 20 years tracking the historical forces that shaped the constitutional crisis I now confronted," writes the late newspaper editor who worked at the center of the story. "Unlike the scores of national correspondents who camped out in our newsroom, I found few surprises in the unfolding events."

"We shattered the mold," recalls a member of the first wave of black reporters to integrate newsrooms. "It didn't matter whether editors were moved by the spirit of the time and took us on out of moral conviction or because they needed African Americans to parachute into urban hot spots too dangerous for white reporters. We were hired, and that was all that mattered."

Media Studies Journal interviews a veteran sportswriter and author about the impact of Muhammad Ali on sports reporting: "He is a very important thread for us, particularly in sports culture and the rise of the black athlete, the rise of the idiosyncratic athlete, the mainstreaming of black style, which has transformed sports."

"Vietnam was a defining moment for American journalism," writes a reporter who covered the war, "because a new generation of war correspondents severed the accommodating relationship their predecessors had forged with the military in two world wars, and instead demanded accountability."

Part IV: The 1970s

A colleague of the slain Ruben Salazar assesses the man's evolving image since his death in 1970: "The canonization of Salazar unfortunately obscured not just the reality of his life but also the significance of his work. Salazar was, above all else, a pro."

"One of the first lessons journalists learned at Wounded Knee, and they came in droves from around the world," writes a Native American journalist, professor and author, "was that they were arriving very late to a story that had deserved their attention much earlier."

"Twenty-five years after the Watergate break-in, American journalism is still recovering from its most celebrated triumph," concludes a television commentator and PBS executive. "It remains the inspiration for a generation of reporters, a justification for journalist intrusion and a paramount example of how the balance of power has shifted from the politicians to the news media."

"I am now a proud member of a craft that today would not grant me entry," reflects the former editor of the *Daily News*. "There is no room in my trade anymore for high school dropouts, or for people without university degrees. That is to say, the city room is no longer open to the likes of Damon Runyon, Jimmy Breslin or Ernest Hemingway."

Part V: The 1980s

A veteran of yesterday's women's sections and today's feature sections writes: "Many of the recent lifestyle sections I've seen appear without purpose. For one, newsrooms steal some of their best ideas, or maybe they are just reclaiming them."

"In the years following Time's merger with Warner, thousands of journalists had to figure out ways to thrive in companies obsessed with show biz," argues a *USA TODAY* columnist. "Newspeople increasingly accept the view that they can serve the public interest by producing stories that interest the public—with subjects for chitchat around the water cooler."

"Every day, all across the country, women sportswriters and broadcasters—and the editors and producers in charge of them—go about their business with no problem," notes a sports reporter for the *Cleveland Plain Dealer*. "In fact, what most of us have found is that the battles now aren't in the field but in the office, where women in sports are facing the same kinds of glass ceilings all women in business face."

Part VI: The 1990s

"Whatever calamitous changes satellite television required, the political system has already shouldered the shock," notes an author and foreign editor of *USA TODAY*. "Call it compassion fatigue or simple inoculation, satellite television has proved to be a sugar high. Once the shock wore off, the pictures lost their punch."

"For centuries rape has been treated as a sideshow in wars," argues an NPR correspondent. "The presence of so many women reporters in Bosnia helped destroy the myth that rape in war was a kind of business as usual."

In the 1992 California primary, an exit poll about a hypothetical candidacy by Ross Perot was deemed more newsworthy than actual primary victories by George Bush and Bill Clinton. "They opened the door to public opinion journalism," writes the director of surveys for CBS News, "and that raised the risk of journalists making up the news."

"With the aid of computers, photographic images will be able to show us much more than just what might present itself at any one time to a well-situated lens," argues an author and journalism professor, "as words tell us about much more than just what is, at any one time, literally the case."

"In Asian-American circles, any discussion of why there are more women in television news is likely to fuel a prickly debate about whether and why Asian-American women are more acceptable to the largely white male news directors who hire them," notes a reporter. "But the question of this gender gap implicates all of us for the simple reason that in television the visual is vital, and an examination of who delivers our news may tell us something about whom we, as a society, have learned to trust."

Part VIII: Review Essay

"The age that nurtured Cronkite, Brinkley and Bradlee represents a fossilized moment of innocence," writes a professor and former CNN producer, "when journalists told us the way it was, and we, more often than not, believed them."

Preface

Two young reporters are roused on a Saturday morning to cover an overnight break-in at an elite Washington address.

A correspondent argues with U.S. military officials about the number of casualties in a battle fought in the mud and half-light of an Asian jungle.

A sportswriter walks into the steam and sweat of a locker room for a postgame interview with the Marquette University men's basketball team.

By themselves, these are not unique scenes in journalism. Fill in some detail and context—the sense of history provided by our contributors—and a different picture emerges. The two young reporters covering the break-in are Bob Woodward and Carl Bernstein in the early stages of Watergate, which, for better and for worse, would become, as Ellen Hume points out, a blueprint for political scandal reporting. The questioning correspondent is Peter Arnett in Vietnam, one of the young reporters whose skepticism about official U.S. reports on the war transformed relations between reporters and the military. And the sportswriter venturing into the locker room is Mary Schmitt, who covered the men's basketball team at Marquette University in the middle 1970s, and in so doing removed one of the last barriers to women's equality in journalism.

These vignettes from news stories are defining moments in the recent history of American journalism because they are part of larger turning points or episodes when American journalists began to think about their work or practice their craft differently.

Of course, when they occurred, none of these episodes appeared to signal cataclysmic change. Most great transformations are not apparent as we live through them. Only in hindsight do individual moments acquire layers of meaning that give them great significance.

Looking back is not something that comes naturally to journalists, immersed as they are in breaking events and relentless deadlines. But there is still good reason for journalists, scholars and people who care about journalism to think about the critical episodes in its recent evolution. The years since the Great Depression and World War II have seen vast changes in America and also in its journalism. Journalists' relationship to power and authority is more complex; the press corps has become more diverse; the technology of news reporting is almost unrecognizably different from that of 50 years ago; and the economic reorganization of the media has bundled news and entertainment organizations into conglomerates of extraordinary size.

Measuring the distance between the past and the present gives a sense of proportion. Pete Hamill's essay on the rise of the white-collar newsroom measures the costs and benefits of the disappearance of the rough and rowdy newsrooms of his youth—which were largely populated by people from immigrant and working-class families. Similarly, Judy Woodruff's essay on women covering politics shows how increased opportunities for women on the political beat have not always been matched by new domestic arrangements that will enable them to take full advantage of workplace opportunities.

While predictions for the future are always uncertain, if you recognize the big forces that are pushing you forward, you can get a rough idea of where you are headed. That's what David Lieberman does in his essay on how the merger of Time and Warner created the uneasy blend of news and show business that many journalists have to live with today.

Finally, a recognition of the often mundane beginnings of big events helps journalists to look for major stories in unexpected places. In this volume, Robert Lipsyte reflects on how a Muhammad Ali press conference in the early 1960s tipped off observant reporters to a new era in sports news and American culture.

The best journalism, after all, reconciles the moment and the process. Reporters who can do that will be ahead of their colleagues and maybe even ahead of the historians. And they will claim a place for themselves in explaining the defining moments in journalism.

—THE EDITORS

Part I

The 1940s

1

The Murrow Boys—
Broadcasting for the Mind's Eye

Stanley Cloud & Lynne Olson

Sixty years ago, the Columbia Broadcasting System, then a struggling network in the still-new business of commercial radio, assigned a promising and ambitious 29-year-old employee named Edward Roscoe Murrow to work in its London office. The title they gave him was "European Director of Talks." His job was to arrange for *others* to go on the air—members of parliament, boys' choirs and the like. As Murrow prepared to sail for England, he was advised by his boss that the 1932 broadcast of a nightingale singing in the Surrey woods, a program that had been chosen by radio's editors as that year's "most interesting," was the standard against which his performance would be judged. Little did anyone know then that Murrow would soon launch a revolution in journalism.

A speech major in college, Edward R. Murrow did not claim to be a journalist and indeed had shown no interest in becoming one. Nor did CBS *want* him to be one. He had worked for international student organizations prior to 1935, the year the network hired him. But he had scarcely unpacked in London two years later before concluding that neither his future nor CBS's lay with nightingales singing in the woods. Europe was headed for a cataclysmic war, Murrow believed, and he was going to find a way to get on the air and report that war for CBS, whether his bosses in New York liked the idea or not.

Up to that point, journalism on radio had consisted primarily of "commentaries" on the news, not reporting. But within a matter of only a few months, Murrow, anticipating the Nazi takeover of Austria, had hired William L. Shirer, an itinerant foreign correspondent then based in Berlin, and had moved him to Vienna. Although New York was still insisting that Murrow and now Shirer act as booking agents, the *Anschluss* in 1938 gave them the break they needed to get on the air.

As Hitler's troops marched into Vienna, the two CBS men provided their listeners with firsthand accounts. They had switched places—Shirer to London, Murrow to Vienna—so that Shirer could have a direct line to New York. With only eight hours' advance warning, he had to arrange for phone lines linking London, Paris, Rome, Berlin and Vienna, and for other reporters and commentators to join him and Murrow on the air. Their amazingly successful broadcast, on March 13, 1938—the first-ever "CBS World News Roundup"—immediately established Murrow and Shirer as bona fide war correspondents. Soon Murrow had hired more young journalists—Eric Sevareid, Larry LeSueur, Tom Grandin, Mary Marvin Breckinridge, Charles Collingwood and several others—and had begun to develop an informal theory about how to report a news story on radio.

The key, he told the members of his team, was to report for the ear, not the eye—or, to put it another way, to report for the *mind's* eye. He wanted his reporters, all of whom he had chosen for their ability to write and think, to imagine themselves standing in front of a fireplace back home, explaining to a group of professional or businesspeople what was happening in Europe. But keep it simple, Murrow said, and tell stories, so that if a maid and her truck-driver boyfriend happen to be eavesdropping, they can understand, too. When Murrow hired Breckinridge, a 33-year-old photojournalist and socialite, and sent her to cover the "phony war" in Amsterdam, he advised: "When you report the invasion of Holland...understate the situation. Don't say the streets are rivers of blood. Say that the little policeman I usually say hello to every morning is not there today."

To some extent, Murrow was borrowing, consciously or unconsciously, from the spare literary and journalistic style established by the likes of Hemingway, Ring Lardner and Mark Twain. But he was the first to adapt that style to the special requirements of radio news. He encouraged analysis and the use of the first person singular, believing that he and his "boys" had the background and firsthand experience to tell their listeners not only what happened but what they thought it meant. Above all, Murrow wanted what he called "pictures in the air," in an era when broadcast reporters were allowed far more airtime to paint such picture stories than are their counterparts today. And what pictures Murrow and the "boys" painted! After Paris was occupied by the Nazis, Sevareid famously reported: "Paris died like a beautiful woman, without struggle, without knowing or even asking why."

Murrow's descriptions of the sights and sounds of the Blitz—inevitably opening with his dramatic "This...is London"—were masterpieces of descriptive reporting. Once during an air raid, Murrow went into Trafalgar Square with his microphone and let his audience listen for a moment to the siren wailing in the background. Then he said, "I'll just ooze down in the darkness alongside these steps and see if I can pick up the sound of people's feet." He laid his mike on the sidewalk, and the click-click of people hurrying for the bomb shelters was carried back to millions of homes in still-neutral America. "One of the strangest sounds one can hear in London these dark nights," Murrow said at last, "is the sound of footsteps along the street, like ghosts shod with steel shoes."

Although Murrow and his team were largely responsible for turning an also-ran network into "the Tiffany's of broadcasting" and for transforming radio generally into a major source of news, their style frequently ran into criticism from the CBS brass in New York. What Murrow and the "boys" thought of as analysis, the brass thought of as "editorializing." The executives were especially worried about incurring further government regulation if CBS's correspondents were perceived by Washington as bucking official U.S. policy. Thus, while the United States was still neutral in the war, the executives wanted CBS to be neutral; but when the United States finally entered the war, they wanted as much flag-waving as possible. Murrow and the others mostly resisted such interference. Sevareid, for example, was scathing—or as scathing as he could be in the face of U.S. military censorship—about the Allies' wasteful and bloody 1944 campaign in Italy.

After the war, the advent of network television drastically altered the nature of electronic reporting. First, so much money and power were at stake in television, and ratings were so important, that the line between news and entertainment became ever more blurry, with devastating effects on quality. Second, good, descriptive writing was gradually de-emphasized. Writing for TV news, with its terrible time constraints, consists mainly of trying to give as many facts as possible as clearly as possible in as few words as possible. That is a not insignificant craft, but today the camera, not the correspondent, is left to paint "pictures in the air." Except for the obsolescent work of journalists in the Charles Kurault "On the Road" mold, the *poetry* of reporting, which Murrow, Sevareid and most of the other "boys" were so good at, has largely been eliminated. As one of the Murrow boys, Charles Collingwood, put it late in his career: "...Today's correspondents so often are limited to writing captions for pictures."

Still, the Murrow legacy is not entirely dead. It lives on in the hearts of countless reporters and producers who, from Vietnam to the Persian Gulf to various toxic-waste dumps, have battled government officials and corporate and political image mongers whose first loyalty is not to the truth but to a particular employer or point of view. In the end, it was the truth, simply told, that Murrow was after. And, against ever greater odds, that is what today's best journalists—on and off the air—are still after.

Stanley Cloud is a former Washington bureau chief, national political correspondent and White House correspondent for Time. *Lynne Olson, a former Moscow correspondent for the AP, teaches at American University. Married, they are the author of* The Murrow Boys *(1996).*

Part II

The 1950s

2

The Lessons of Little Rock

Harry S. Ashmore

By labor day 1957, when Gov. Orval Faubus suddenly deployed the
Arkansas National Guard to prevent the invasion of Little Rock's Central High School by nine black children, I had spent 20 years tracking
the historical forces that shaped the constitutional crisis I now confronted as executive editor of the *Arkansas Gazette*.

Unlike the scores of national correspondents who camped out in our
newsroom, I found few surprises in the unfolding events that kept Little
Rock at the top of the news over the next two years. But I found much
to regret as superficial media treatment branded the city with a reputa-
tion of bigotry it didn't deserve.

I had already acquired a brand of my own as one of the handful of
Southern journalists identified as liberal in the national press. Upon
my appointment as editor of the *Charlotte News* in 1947, *Time* had
cited me as "one of the South's most realistic and readable editorial
writers." But, in seeking to place me in the political spectrum, it had
been necessary to add a regional discount:

> His campaigns (for two-party politics, racial and religious tolerance, votes for
> Negroes, higher pay for teachers) have established him as neither a Yankee-lover
> nor a deep-dyed Southerner. Ashmore tempers his enthusiasm for reform with
> consideration for the facts of Southern life.... Says he: "I am a Southerner by
> inclination as well as by virtue of two Confederate grandfathers, but it is high
> time we rejoined the union."

The dominant fact of Southern life was the existence of a social order
openly based on the doctrine of white supremacy. Legally enforced
segregation of the races had survived the abolition of slavery and was
now embodied in a one-party political system that disenfranchised blacks
and severely limited their ability to rise above their assigned place at
the bottom of the class structure.

As a fledgling political writer in my native South Carolina, I had seen the inherent injustices of the system highlighted in the course of the New Deal effort to repair the ravages of the Great Depression. But those of us who pointed out gross inequities in the distribution of benefits to blacks were open to charges of apostasy—an indictment still potent enough to prompt most newspapers to indulge in traditional tirades against meddling outsiders. The rest usually maintained a prudent silence.

For my generation of Southerners, fealty to the shibboleths of the Old South was undermined by the global conflict of World War II that sent most of us to far places. I had no illusion that the veterans had come home imbued by a passion for reform, but at Charlotte I found that the *News* could attract considerable support for a reasoned argument for racial justice—meaning equality before the law—as long as there was no implication of social equality between blacks and whites.

But that kind of editorial straddling was no longer possible after 1948, when President Truman announced his support for a package of civil rights legislation that would require the final dismantling of the South's peculiar institutions. I would face the new test of Southern sentiment at the *Gazette*, a venerable morning paper that, like the *News*, was owned by a patrician family with roots deep in the region.

In 50 years as president and editor, the erudite J.N. Heiskell had endowed the newspaper with an institutional character, paid tribute in a memoir by James Street, a Mississippi author who had apprenticed there. The newspaper's respect for tradition, he wrote, was that of a genteel Southern lady, "her Confederate limbs hidden under a Victorian petticoat and seen only in stormy weather when she kicks up her heels in an eye-catching crusade for her principles."

Those occasions had arisen when demagogues sought to exploit race prejudice. Heiskell's view was similar to that expressed by Harry Truman during his service as U.S. senator from Missouri, when he identified the issue as one of justice, not social equality. And Heiskell had no disposition to challenge the verdict of history when Truman, as president, concluded that justice could not be done under a binding system that enforced separation of the races without providing the corollary equality of treatment. The *Gazette* thus became one of the few major Southern newspapers likely to hire an editor with the views I had voiced at Charlotte.

I found myself in the eye of a political hurricane when Ben Laney, then governor of Arkansas, emerged as chairman from the founding meeting of the States' Rights Jeffersonian Democrats with a manifesto that declared:

> the President of the United States has by his acts and declarations repudiated the principles of the Democratic Party, threatened to disturb the constitutional division and balance of the powers of government, and has thereby forfeited all claims of allegiance from members of the party who adhere to its principles.

The Democratic National Convention nominated Truman after a young Minnesota delegate named Hubert Humphrey declared on the floor, "The time has come for the Democratic Party to get out of the shadow of states' rights and walk forthrightly into the bright sunshine of human rights." When the dissident Southern Democrats reconvened in Birmingham, Ala., to formally launch a "Dixiecrat" third party, Laney, a gentlemanly conservative, stepped aside in favor of a Dixiecrat ticket headed by the uninhibited Strom Thurmond of South Carolina, with Fielding Wright of Mississippi as his running mate.

The *Gazette* had nailed the Democratic banner to its masthead when it was founded in 1819, and, as we rolled out the editorial artillery in support of the straight party ticket headed by President Truman, I asked "Mr. J.N.," as everyone called him, if the newspaper had ever been anything other than Democratic. "I don't like to talk about this," he said, "but the fact is we went Whig twice."

In the end the rebellious faction carried only four states in the Deep South, and I wrote what I hoped would be an obituary for the Dixiecrat movement:

> Although they tried to be polite about it, it was quite clear that they were in fact the anti-Negro party.... The case they presented to the Southern voter was a familiar one. They appealed to his prejudices and played upon his fears. They hurled the reckless charge that election of either major candidate would mean Negro domination of the South, and for good measure added the allegation that the civil rights program endorsed by both the Democrats and Republicans is Communist in nature and inspiration.

The package of civil rights legislation that touched off the rebellion got nowhere when Truman sent it to Congress. But the U.S. Supreme Court was steadily whittling away the states' rights doctrine in cases brought by the NAACP, and in the 1950s it set down for argument cases calling for desegregation of public education from kindergarten through graduate school.

Drafted by the Fund for the Advancement of Education to summarize scholarly studies on the effect of the pending decision, I completed my report in time for the University of North Carolina Press to publish it on the eve of the landmark *Brown* decision, handed down in 1954. When I told an old Arkansas politician that I was writing a book called *The Negro and the Schools*, he bespoke the conventional wisdom: "Son, it sounds to me like you have gotten yourself in the position of a man running for sonofabitch without opposition."

The Court's unanimous decision mandating an end to the dual school system produced a roar of outrage in the Deep South, but in the upper tier states, public officials—including Gov. Faubus—indicated that they would support compliance. In Little Rock, when the city's school board announced the immediate initiation of a comprehensive plan to desegregate the schools, it had the support of both newspapers, an alliance of ministers and the Chamber of Commerce.

But it was soon evident that elected officials could not prevail against mounting pressure for massive resistance without moral support from Washington, and none was forthcoming. As the 1956 national election approached, I was convinced that the erosion of popular support for compliance could not be halted without the election of a president who understood Southern politics and could command the support of the loyal Democrats who still dominated the political process in most Southern states.

I had come to know and admire Gov. Adlai Stevenson of Illinois when he ran for president in 1952. A classic WASP with a family that included cousins scattered across Dixie, he had a natural talent for reconciliation. When he indicated willingness to run again, I took leave from the *Gazette* to serve as his personal assistant in the 1956 presidential campaign.

This was the first national election in which candidates were nominated in party primaries, and it followed that it was the first in which television played a dominant role. But the sporadic coverage of grassroots campaigning provided no context for the hundreds of speeches Stevenson made as he carried out his pledge to talk sense to the American people, culminating in the demand that his opponent face up to what surely should have been a defining campaign issue:

> The presidency is above all a place of moral leadership. Yet in these months of crucial importance no leadership has been provided. The immense prestige and influence of the office has been withheld from those who honestly seek to carry out the law in a gathering storm and against rising resistance. Refusing to rise to this great moral and constitutional crisis, the administration had hardly acknowledged its gravity.

President Eisenhower simply ignored Stevenson's challenge. As a military hero he had been swept into office without political baggage, and television made it possible to substitute image for substance. The comforting appearance on the home screens of a benign, avuncular figure who had served his country well in time of war was enough to stifle partisan controversy.

After his landslide victory, Eisenhower made no secret of his personal disapproval of school desegregation. The politician he admired most, he confided, was Harry F. Byrd of Virginia, an unreconstructed apostle of states' rights. He refused to use his office to lend moral support to the Supreme Court, and said of Brown's principal architect, "The worst damn fool mistake I made was appointing Earl Warren chief justice."

As it had in the election campaign, television proved to be a determinant in shaping the popular response to the inevitable constitutional crisis that followed a year later. Harry Reasoner, one of the young legmen the TV networks dispatched to Arkansas when rioting broke out at Central High, cited Little Rock as the place "where television came to influence, if not to maturity."

The coaxial cable had spread from coast to coast, making it possible for the networks to project motion pictures from the scene of a news event into 50 million homes. This struck David Halberstam as the most significant development of the decade he chronicled in *The Fifties*. The images captured by TV cameras at Central High were "so forceful they told their own truths and needed virtually no narration...."

> It was hard for people watching at home not to take sides. They were sitting in their living rooms in front of their own television sets watching orderly black children behaving with great dignity, trying to obtain nothing more than a decent education, the most elemental of American birthrights, yet being assaulted by a vicious mob of poor whites.

In that sense, Little Rock was a defining moment for the new visual medium—and for the civil rights movement that found its moral appeal greatly enhanced by the dramatic display of racist brutality.

But equal treatment for the black minority was, as it had been since the founding of the republic, a political as well as a moral issue, and its ramifications could not be fully understood without the historical context TV proved unable to provide. In the excitement of the moment, it was possible to ignore the broader implications of the front-page editorial I wrote for the *Gazette*:

> ...the issue is no longer segregation vs. integration. The question has now become the supremacy of the government of the United States in all matters of

law. And clearly the federal government cannot let this issue remain unresolved
no matter what the cost to this community.

Although he was motivated not by ideology but by simple expediency,
Gov. Faubus' challenge to federal authority was mounted in the name
of states' rights. In the former Confederacy, the Supreme Court's *Brown*
decision represented what Justice Felix Frankfurter called "the intrusion of a distant voice," and it invoked the folk memory of a lost war.
That could be met only by a forcible reminder that the issue of federal
supremacy had been settled 100 years ago.

The enduring importance of Little Rock lay in the forcing of
Eisenhower's hand. Faced with the use of state military forces to defy
his government's courts, the president had no option but to send in his
own troops to restore and maintain order. His effort to temporize with
Gov. Faubus and the intransigent governors in the Deep South had
failed in a fashion that affirmed the commitment of the federal executive to guarantee the constitutional rights of black citizens wherever,
and however, they might be denied.

This made possible the nonviolent protest Martin Luther King Jr.
led against demeaning Jim Crow laws that denied blacks access to places
of public accommodation and gainful employment. When thousands
of freedom marchers took to the streets, they were no longer at the
mercy of local authorities, the mobs they often encouraged and the
state courts that were usually rigged against them—and TV cameras
were on hand to provide a close-up view of last-ditch skirmishing among
the ruins of the old segregated society.

By 1964, Lyndon Johnson, the Southern Democrat who succeeded
the martyred John F. Kennedy was able to rally a national consensus
in support of affirmative federal action to deal with the last vestiges
of legal segregation. By that time I had been rehabilitated, ultimately
receiving honorary degrees from Clemson, the South Carolina alma
mater I shared with Strom Thurmond, and the University of Arkansas. When the latter was announced, a former colleague at the *Gazette* called to tell me, "We're all sitting around trying to figure out
who had to be dead before this could happen."

But the consensus began to unravel three years later when mob
violence erupted in a poor black community in Los Angeles. The TV
cameras were there in Watts too, and they followed along as looting
and arson spread across the country to a hundred inner cities, all of
them outside the South. The spectacle of militant black youths defy-
ing law enforcement authorities in their own bailiwick profoundly

affected those who had cherished the illusion that the corrosive effects of racial prejudice were confined to the benighted region below the Mason-Dixon Line.

The nation emerged from the Long Hot Summers with its traditional partisan division reshaped by the revival of states' rights doctrine, now being advocated by those who professed to be free of racist sentiment. The Republican Party seized upon it as a means of reducing the taxing and regulatory authority of the central government, and President Richard Nixon devised the "Southern strategy" that finally split the once-solid regional bastion that had given the Democratic Party at least nominal control of Congress.

The ideological conflict among whites had its counterpart among blacks. Militant leaders rejected Martin Luther King's integrationist goal and advocated a separate black community as a means of preserving professed Afrocentric values. The kind of emotion-laden controversy that divided both races, and set them against each other, met the histrionic demands of television and thereby became a prime factor in halting the forward progress of the civil rights movement before it reached the poor blacks huddled below the poverty line.

Little Rock had demonstrated that rhetorical violence inevitably begets the real thing, but the lesson was largely ignored as race-baiting became a standard means of discrediting social programs that for 50 years had provided a safety net for those unable to earn a subsistence income. However, the residual effect of the nation's heritage of racism, and the necessity of federal intervention to deal with it, had been indelibly impressed upon an up-and-coming politician from Arkansas who had been a student at Hot Springs Junior High School when the 101st Airborne Infantry landed at Little Rock. As president, Bill Clinton cited Martin Luther King Jr. as the teacher of his generation of Southerners and proclaimed reconciliation as the leitmotif of his second term.

But after 40 years of one-dimensional treatment of social issues by the media, which seizes upon conflict without proper regard for context or cause, it remained to be seen whether the lessons of Little Rock still could be impressed upon the national consciousness.

The late Harry S. Ashmore, a Pulitzer-Prize winner for editorial writing, was the executive editor of the Little Rock Arkansas Gazette. *He was author or editor of 14 books on public service, including a new edition of* Civil Rights and Wrongs *(1997).*

Part III
The 1960s

3

The Black Vanguard Integrates Newsrooms

Paul Delaney

We were young and hardy, recently out of college. In our search for jobs we stared down Jim Crow, undaunted by the resistance we ran into at every editor's desk. We were cocky, too, to the bone. But best of all, we were certifiably ready, degrees in hand, as qualified as our white classmates who graduated with us but whose careers were jump-started immediately into totally white newsrooms. No dues paying for those guys.

In the 1950s and early 1960s we were the vanguard, the first generation of African-American reporters to integrate newsrooms and get those reporting jobs as real journalists. It was no accident that newsroom integration paralleled the national push for integration. Editors were very aware of the contradiction of condemning racism, especially in the South, and not dealing with it closer to home, on their staffs. Yet even though the members of the vanguard generation fought the good fight in their own time, and the civil rights era gave way to movements by women and other groups, serious racial problems persist to this day inside newsrooms, just as they persist in the country that surrounds them. Young minority journalists face some of the same roadblocks we faced back then.

Before we broke in, the tradition at the few daily newspapers that hired African Americans at all was to carry a Negro page that ran on Saturday's back page, usually, "edited" by a black nonjournalist who was forced to shuffle through the back door with social and church items. That was it for news about us, except for crime and briefs that gave whites a chuckle.

Not us. Not the vanguard. We shattered the mold. We had equipped ourselves by training at some of the best journalism programs and campus newspapers. When dailies were finally ready for us, we were fiercely ready for them. It didn't matter whether editors were moved by the spirit of the time and took us on out of moral conviction or because they needed African Americans to parachute into urban hot spots too dangerous for white reporters. We were hired, and that was all that mattered.

A white editor interviewing me and trying to appear earnest, looked me straight in the eyes and declared, "Don't think we're hiring you because you're black." Without blinking and trying not to laugh in his face, I shot back, "And I wouldn't take the job if that's the reason you want me." It was poker, like much else about our entry into white newsrooms.

In some cases, the media were pressured to integrate. In the mid-'60s, tension in many big cities was as thick and acrid as smoke from burning car tires. Eventually, protests and rioting sprang from tightly wound race relations. In Washington, D.C., in 1967, the Student Non-Violent Coordinating Committee (SNCC) proclaimed that, henceforth, only blacks would be allowed to cover the organization's press conferences and meetings. The *Washington Star*, where I worked along with two other black reporters, Ernest Holsendolph and Paul Hathaway, had no problems; nor did the *Washington Post*, with more nonwhites than just about any other news company. But the *Washington Daily News* and some radio and television stations, complaining bitterly, had to scramble to hire African-American reporters. SNCC had called the media's hand and won.

We in the vanguard were dedicated, talented and loyal to the profession. We were serious and hardworking. And we were as ambitious as the next guy, the white guy. No different from today's young minority journalists. In retrospect, however, little did we know that management was not inclined to promote us all the way to the top, or even near it in most cases. We were oh, so naive, too—although not entirely without reason.

When I became the first black reporter at the *Dayton* (Ohio) *Daily News* in 1963, any prior resistance to newsroom integration seemed to melt at the door. It was, indeed, an "era of good feeling." I was welcomed with open arms. Years later I learned that a reporter who opposed my hiring declared when I arrived, "There's that black bastard." Before I was told the story, she had become one of my drinking buddies, biggest boosters and best friends on the paper. I was hired as a general assignment reporter and eventually covered the courts. Yet the editor, Jim Fain, refused to assign me to civil rights stories. I had to fight to write about Dayton's black community. Fain did not want me pigeonholed as his "black" reporter.

The entry of most of the vanguard was as syrupy as the pop songs of the period. I remember swaying with my white colleagues to the strains of Petula Clark's "Downtown" at the same time whites were streaming out of America's downtown.

In the euphoria of breaking barriers, we momentarily forgot that the Great Emancipator and Reconstruction were followed by Jim Crow. Newsroom integration was mostly in the North. The South was a different story. No Emancipation there for a couple more decades. No one paid much attention, but the newsroom of the *Atlanta Constitution*, where Ralph McGill held forth so famously on behalf of civil rights, was never truly integrated during his tenure.

After we covered the riots, we set about trying to influence not only the racial makeup of the newsroom, but also its thinking about the nonwhite outside and the culture inside. We wanted editors to factor nonwhites into every facet of the news operation. I was in meetings at the *Times*, for example, where artists were told to include obviously nonwhite faces in their drawings, to get away from the idea that the world is made up solely of white people.

Newsrooms really did begin to change for the better. Our numbers increased substantially and substantively. (Mind you, it was only four years ago that the annual survey of the American Society of Newspaper Editors could show that newsrooms with nonwhite professionals had finally tipped past the 50 percent mark.) The percentage of minorities in the newsroom is now 18 percent, with nonwhite managers making up 11 percent.

We eventually came to understand that we would have difficulty winning the prime jobs in journalism as publishers, editors, bureau chiefs and desk heads. A handful did make it early on, in the 1970s: Bob Maynard at the *Washington Post* and eventually publisher of the *Oakland* (Calif.) *Tribune*; Al Fitzpatrick at the *Akron* (Ohio) *Beacon-Journal*. Quite a few of us advanced later in the 1980s and 1990s. A few major chains, including Gannett and Knight Ridder, made it their business to push nonwhites upward, under the leadership of men at the top who decided it was time to go beyond window-dressing.

In my own case, after working at the *Dayton Daily News* and *Washington Star*, I was hired onto the *New York Times*' Washington bureau and eventually worked in the Chicago and Madrid bureaus and as an editor on the national desk. My start at the *Times* was fairly easy, coming after an amazing stint as a city hall reporter at the *Star*, where my partner, Ron Sarro, and I beat the daylight out of the *Post* with almost daily scoops. True, I was the first black in the elite Washington bureau, but there were other African Americans at the *Times*: Charlayne Hunter, Tom Johnson, Nancy Hicks and Gerald Frazier in New York, Earl Caldwell in San Francisco, plus a few photographers and copy editors, though none of us with any real power or authority. I eventually became an editor on the national news desk as the numbers of reporters, and in time other professionals, increased significantly. Among our colleagues and in the black community, being The Few brought us great status and responsibility.

Tension between the races in the newsroom began in the 1970s as more nonwhites were hired, posing a threat—or perceived threat—to white males. Traditional newsroom rivalry turned into antagonism— sometimes madness—in the 1980s, helped along by Reagan administration anti-civil rights policies and politics that extended even to journalists. Racial tension was also fueled by the advent of a few right-wing ideologues in newsrooms—or at least their coming out of the closet in protests against minority hiring and promotion. A colleague at the *Times* was writing an article on the hostility in the mid-1980s and characterized it as "racial guerrilla warfare." I discouraged him from the description, but later thought that, perhaps, I should not have.

Today, young, talented minority professionals and prospective journalists are not as patient, nor forgiving, as we were. Some gifted prospects either leave the field in frustration or avoid it altogether. They do not like to hear those of us from the vanguard preach patience, but most of them accord us respect and appreciate our counsel. We see each other often, at NABJ conventions and at other functions.

The battle to integrate newsrooms is far from over. The same polarization that poisons the nation is found in the media, an institution that should exploit its influence and provide leadership. The pursuit of diversity, with the goal of integration, is still extremely controversial in the newsroom. Yet, the presence of nonwhite editors and reporters has had a profound effect. Most dailies and television news now routinely run features on African Americans and other people of color.

The baton is passed. A new generation will have to face the old problems in its own way. The youngsters will do it differently, of course. A few years ago, a group tried to form an under-35 branch of the NABJ, feeling the outlook of the vanguard was outdated, viewed from the 1960s. The effort failed. Maybe not the next time. But it's their call; they are now the vanguard.

Paul Delaney, one of the first black editors and a former reporter for the New York Times, *is the former chairman of the University of Alabama's department of journalism. He is currently editorial page editor of* Our World News (OWN).

4

Covering Ali, Discovering an Era

Robert Lipsyte

The story of the boxer Muhammad Ali, which transcends the misleading distinctions between sports, politics and culture, stretches from the tumult of the 1960s to the muddles of the 1990s. Robert Lipsyte, who has written about Ali since his earliest days, talked to Robert W. Snyder of *Media Studies Journal* about his experiences covering "the Greatest."

MSJ: You've argued that the Muhammad Ali story compelled American sportswriters to make a connection between sports and society and politics. Was there a moment or an episode when you recognized that Ali was having that effect on sportswriting?

ROBERT LIPSYTE: Certainly my consciousness that something had happened was the morning right after he beat Liston.

We're talking February 1964. The Vietnam War was heating up. There was a disproportionate number of blacks going to war. The Muslims, the black Muslims as they were called, did not allow their members to join the army.

Malcolm X was scaring whites. It was a front-page story, bigger than Louis Farrakhan now. And within boxing, which is a sport that has always been very closely tied to organized crime and state and city legislature, there was a real fear that blacks would economically take over.

Also, there was kind of a generational thing going on in sportswriting. The younger reporters—I was in my early 20s at the time—were excited by Ali. And then he won, which he was not supposed to do.

Next morning there was a press conference, and Liston was uncharacteristically gentlemanly. Of course, he had a return-bout contract. And Ali was uncharacteristically quiet. And he said: 'Now, I can be a gentleman; the whole thing was just for show. It was just a fraud, it was just to get people into the tent. Now I can be a good, decent guy.'

At that moment, all the older reporters left to file their stories. And the younger reporters said, 'No, no, no, this just doesn't sound right.' And what we were interested in was whether he was really a member of the Nation of Islam.

I think the question that set him off was, 'Are you a card-carrying Muslim?'

And he said, 'What does that mean, card-carrying Muslim? I'm decent. I don't smoke, I don't drink. I don't sleep with your women. What's the big deal? Don't you understand, in this world, which is a jungle, the red birds have to stay with red birds, and the blue birds with blue birds.'

And he made an absolute case for segregation. People have to stay with their own, they shouldn't go where they're not wanted.

And then, somebody said, 'Well, how can you say this, after Jackie Robinson and Joe Louis, what people have fought for?'

And he said, 'I don't have to be who you want me to be. I'm free to be who I want.' And that was the athletic declaration of independence.

No athlete had ever said that so publicly before. American athletes had always been more or less sweet-tempered killers who worked for the establishment....

MSJ: Did sportswriters know at the time that something had happened?

ROBERT LIPSYTE: We knew that something had happened. Jackie Robinson never said that, and certainly if there is a hero in American sports, a singular individual, you would pick Robinson.

But Ali said that he was free. And I think, at that moment, the impact was enormous because what this ultimately led to was when he refused to step forward [and be inducted into the armed forces], which was an absolute extension of being free to be who you are. He believed in his religion, believed in his right as an American. So when that happened, I think it became necessary to cover him in a different way. To many people it then became necessary to cover him in a very specifically negative political way.

MSJ: Was there a generational dimension to that?

ROBERT LIPSYTE: The really important sportswriters of the previous generation—Jimmy Cannon, Red Smith and Arthur Daly—and their clones all around the country attacked Ali out of a World War II patriotic sensibility.

Also, there had been a tremendous amount of agitation about bringing up black baseball players. And a lot of it came from those older sportswriters, especially Cannon. He had fought that battle. And he saw this clown—now that I see it from a distance, not without some justification—chipping away at what he thought they had accomplished.

Here was Ali saying red birds should stay with red birds when Cannon had put his career on the line to say that Joe Louis was a credit to his race, the human race.... Now here comes Ali, and he's a black Muslim, he's against integration, he's against Martin Luther King. He's a bad guy.

MSJ: Yet, as you've written many times, he became beatified.

ROBERT LIPSYTE: He paid the price. I don't think that there's anything that convinces Americans more of sincerity than when you lose a lot of money. He lost a lot of money.

MSJ: And that registered with reporters too?

ROBERT LIPSYTE: Oh, yeah. We saw how much money he lost. This is a man who never got a major corporate endorsement. He did Roach Motel. Think about it. Never did a car, never did a soft drink. Amazing.

So he lost a lot of money. He was sincere. He was totally sincere. The other thing was, of course, that he became nonthreatening. Sweet shuffler. Can't talk. He smiles, he hugs, he makes you cry....

MSJ: What role did Howard Cosell play in making Ali both famous and accepted?

ROBERT LIPSYTE: Well, Howard, although he was of the older generation, was really a new kid on the block—a pioneer in what's really very common now—the total integration of news and entertainment about sports on television.

And he was a lawyer, he was smarter than everybody else, and he had a conscience. And while he was basically a conservative person in every way, he really believed in the Constitution, both as a lawyer and as a minority member, a Jew.

He had been in World War II, he had been an army officer, he had credentials. And he saw that this guy, besides being a ride to the top for him and his career—which is not to be forgotten—was also being persecuted.

So Cosell was critical. Cosell kept him alive during all the years of the exile. Cosell gave him a humorous face on television.

MSJ: To what extent did Ali play the press to get the kind of coverage that he wanted?

ROBERT LIPSYTE: He was about the best. He could unerringly know what you wanted—whether you were simpering, bleeding-heart, pseudointellectual liberal, like myself, or if you were a right-wing asshole, like Dick Young.

Dick Young could walk into the gym and Ali would say, 'There he is, the most dangerous man in America! Strong men quake, women quiver when Dick Young comes to write.'

How could Dick Young not be totally thrilled? The same with Jimmy Cannon.

And he could do that to everybody. He could tell whether you wanted to be serious or not. I was, for many years, in a serious mode, so he was serious with me. It was fun and it was easy.

Let's not forget, that you could land in a city at 6 o'clock, take a cab to where Ali was, meet him at 6:30 and know that you were going to make your 7:30 deadline. You'd get something in an hour. Even if he gave you a hard time.

MSJ: Which medium was better suited to Ali, print or television?

ROBERT LIPSYTE: Television was better for him because you could see how pretty he was. And what amazes people when they see Ali is how big he is. On television, you don't get the sense of his size because he's so perfectly proportioned. And he was funny and he could be nice. And warm. And he was very compassionate. He was a really good guy. He was the kind of guy who would be late for a plane and would stop in an airport so some old woman could take his photograph, and then realize that her lens cap was on, gently take it off and suggest she do it again, because she wouldn't want to miss this moment.

MSJ: Did you see him do that?

ROBERT LIPSYTE: Yeah, I've been with him when he did that. He almost missed the plane. And I had to file. And he'd read in a story about some Jewish home for the aged going down, and he'd cry and run over there and give them a $100,000 check.

MSJ: Did you see that?

ROBERT LIPSYTE: Yeah. He was capable of this sort of thing. He was not a mean-spirited man. A lot of athletes tend to be ordinary people with extraordinary skills. And he was an extraordinary person, as well. He was beautiful. He was a genius at what he was.

MSJ: There seems to be a kind of paradox to him. On the one hand, he's anti-racist, but he calls Joe Frazier a gorilla. He also says things that some liberals would find sexist and anti-gay. You wrote recently about how he's all for harmony but he jokes to reporters that the difference between canoes and Jews is that Jews don't tip. Are reporters covering for him?

ROBERT LIPSYTE: Totally. Actually, he's kind of run by iconographers now. He's not really being covered—he's being beatified. Access is carefully given. I think I'm on the outs now. It's happened before. I go out of favor, and then a couple of years pass, and I'm allowed back in again.

The first time it happened was in '75. I was doing a *Times* magazine piece. We were leaving a ball field at Daytona Beach, Fla. He'd given an exhibition. The recreational vehicle that he had used as his dressing room was cleared out. We were all headed back to the airport, and he pulled two women out of the crowd and locked the door of the recreational vehicle, and it started shaking.

And all his handlers said: 'You didn't see that, you didn't see that. You must never write that or he'll never talk with you again.' And by that time, I figured I would never talk to him again, anyway. I didn't care. And I wrote just that.

Everybody said, 'Well, you blew that, too bad, because he was really good for your career.' And the title of the piece when it ran was 'The King of All Kings.' I saw him a year and a half later. And he grabbed me and said, 'Hey, that's great. You really showed them what a king of all kings I really am!'

MSJ: Why did most journalists not cover it then?

ROBERT LIPSYTE: Because they figured that it would deny them access. He was an easy story....

MSJ: You wrote that as Ali gets older, he makes cynicism impossible. But this sounds to me like a cynical arrangement.

ROBERT LIPSYTE: I'm not cynical about it at all. I think it's wrong. I think cynicism is when you accept it. I'm not accepting it. I'm very skeptical of the way we cover him, or the way we cover politicians.

A cynical arrangement, is when a lot of people have made pragmatic arrangements in order to ensure access....

He is a very important thread for us, particularly in sports culture and the rise of the black athlete, the rise of the idiosyncratic athlete, the mainstreaming of black style, which has transformed sports.

MSJ: What's that done for sports journalism?

ROBERT LIPSYTE: It's created some real problems for sports journalism. To a large extent, it's only recently that there are enough black reporters, black working-class reporters, if there are any, who can talk about this in any kind of accurate way.

It's been a real strain on journalism because sports journalism has always lagged behind what capital J journalism thinks it's about. I'm not so sure about capital J journalism, but I do know that sports journalism has had a very difficult time deciding whether you're covering news or whether you are extending the pleasure of the entertainment for your readers. Are you a movie reviewer? Or are you a street reporter?

And this is complicated when there seem to be real conflicts and tensions within sports between a white hierarchy and a black player constituency with very, very different goals.

Sports also is in transition from being a moral crucible for America to being just another theme park, just another entertainment, which complicates the reporter's life even more. We are now guides in Disneyland when once we thought we were somewhere between being real reporters and moral arbiters.

MSJ: I was looking at all the coverage of Ali in the opening ceremony of the '96 Olympics. Is he going to become a conventional celebrity for people?

ROBERT LIPSYTE: Well, he has. He's going to the opening of envelopes now. I see him all over the place. And I think that's how he's making his money. I don't think that he's poverty-stricken, but he certainly doesn't have as much money as he should have.

He dresses up a place. It's like having a Mother Teresa photo-op. He lends something to the proceedings, without saying anything. He evokes whatever it is you want him to evoke. Whatever it is that's the best in your nature, he evokes.

MSJ: A friend of mine said that Ali's popularity with liberals had less to do with what he really believed and more with the people he opposed.

ROBERT LIPSYTE: I think that's accurate.

MSJ: Are there things that you learned in writing about him over the years that you would like to transmit to people who are starting to write about sports today?

ROBERT LIPSYTE: The most important thing that I learned was never to save anything for future access. Whatever you've got, go with it. You've got to write what you see, when you see it, not with the idea that if you hold it back now you'll get access when the really big, important story comes. Because when the really big, important story comes, they will call up Harold Evans and sell it to Random House.

MSJ: You did that with Ali, and yet he always seems to welcome you back.

ROBERT LIPSYTE: Yeah, that's what I learned. Of course, had I been a city hall reporter, I would be out on my ass. And had I been a business reporter, I'd be dead. But I guess it was OK in sports. They weren't killing people in sports. Then.

I remember once, after the Liston/Ali fights, there were Senate hearings on boxing and there was a purge. And one of the shadowy figures was a Las Vegas hustler named Ash Resnick.

I wrote about him as this well-dressed, handsome, vile shit who should be run out of sports and was a stain on boxing. If boxing could possibly be stained, this man would do it.

About six months later, I was in Vegas covering a fight, and I cut through a dark parking lot to get to my car, which I had cheaply not valet parked. And all of a sudden, Resnick and two guys, two gorillas, leaped in front of me. And Resnick grabbed me by the shirt. And he pulled me up really close to him and these two gorillas were on either side, and he said, 'Handsome, huh?' And let me go. Go figure.

Robert Lipsyte is a sports and city columnist for the New York Times.

5

Vietnam and War Reporting

Peter Arnett

Roberts Field, Liberia—This place feels like wartime Vietnam, the humid air ripened by the rotting smell from thick jungle that curls over the edges of the airstrip, the odor spiced with acrid exhaust fumes belched by arriving U.S. Air Force C-130 Troop transports. Further adding to the illusion, a U.S. Special Forces A Team shouts instructions to a company of Ghanian troops running from the planes to waiting vehicles. The Ghanians are there to beef up a West African military force guiding Liberia towards elections that may bring an end to the vicious civil war. And the U.S. military is helping out with the logistics.

Sound like the Vietnamese Central Highlands, circa 1964? It's even the same latitude. But more than 30 years later, it's definitely not the same attitude. As we climb off one of the arriving aircraft, I hear above the roar of the idling engines the shouted, "Jesus Christ, CNN!" The A Team commander is convinced that our unexpected presence at Roberts Field will unduly excite a crowd of locals gathered to bid farewell to a departing politician. It might jeopardize his mission. We are unceremoniously bundled into a helicopter with the colonel explaining, "It's better for all of us that you stay out of the way." We are quickly airborne and outta there.

Stay out of the way? In Vietnam no one treated us like that. We were always in the way. We made a point of it. But the colonel didn't know that. He later told me he entered military service a year after the war ended. But he did know that in Pentagon war games in recent years, media presence on the battlefield was considered an unpredictable factor to be worried about, like the weather. So he worried.

Blame it on Vietnam. That's when the military learned to worry about the media. Vietnam was a defining moment for American journalism because a new generation of war correspondents severed the accommodating relationship their predecessors had forged with the military in two world wars, and instead demanded accountability.

When I was assigned to Saigon in June 1962, as an AP correspondent, bureau chief Mal Browne was hopping mad with the Vietnamese and American authorities, and complained he'd been repeatedly misled and lied to about the military buildup. One example of the cavalier attitude: When Browne called the U.S. Embassy to ask about the unannounced arrival of a score of helicopters on the docks in front of the Majestic Hotel, he was told he was seeing things, that they didn't exist.

What Browne and the rest of us were doing was revealing policy decisions—which Washington wanted concealed—about vastly increased military assistance and expanded rules of engagement that required American soldiers to use their weapons. Such decisions were pushing the United States deeper into the conflict. We believed the American public had the right to know about these things.

And U.S. officials blatantly tried to cover up battlefield disasters. When David Halberstam and I hitched a ride to cover the aftermath of the battle of Ap Bac in early January 1963, we saw that it had clearly been a Viet Cong victory—the most significant action of the war up to that time. We encountered the senior American commander, Gen. Paul D. Harkins, at the bloody scene who said with a straight face, "We've got them in a trap and we're going to spring it in half an hour." Then he immediately left the place. Around that time, the Pacific Fleet commander, Adm. Harry Felt, personally castigated the Saigon press corps for our critical reporting and demanded that we "get on the team." Little wonder there were no takers.

The official American antagonism towards the press played into the hands of the autocratic administration of President Ngo Dinh Diem. Diem's security forces pummeled and arrested not only Vietnamese critics of the regime but, on one occasion, Mal Browne and me, threatening us with charges of espionage—punishable by death. The assault on the regime's critics and the Saigon press corps bonded us together and cast a harsh spotlight on America's policy of "sink or swim with Ngo Dinh Diem." As more Buddhist monks immolated themselves on Saigon streets, the administration of President John F. Kennedy decided to change horses, and by year's end an American-backed *coup d'état* had swept the Diem regime into history.

Attempts by officials to restrict the flow of negative news from Vietnam were equally as difficult on the battlefield when American combat troops arrived as they were in the streets of Saigon when the Buddhists rioted. The American soldiers did not look upon the press as a fifth column of spies. For the first few years of the war they were zealous and self-assured and proud of what they were doing, and willing to talk openly about it. We had many quarrels with officials in Saigon and Washington over the years, but we rarely clashed with servicemen in the field from the advisers through to combat forces. Even though Brig. Gen. Ellis Williamson, the commander of the elite U.S. Army 173rd Airborne Brigade, disliked me personally because of stories I had written about the skills of the Viet Cong when facing his troops, his attempts to ban me from his outfit failed because his unit commanders kept smuggling me onto the operational helicopters. Whatever the general's opinions, his soldiers were happy to get my attention.

The view of Vietnam from the trenches was not a pretty one, and the American commander, Gen. William C. Westmoreland, made it clear in bureau chief briefings that my kind of field reporting, from the heart of the action, was unacceptable to him. He complained that for the first time in the history of warfare, news reports were going directly from the infantry squad to the American public before the area commander even knew what was going on. The general argued that the morale of troops in the field and the folks at home had to be considered, and a positive approach needed to be taken.

My own news organization, the AP, wrestled with the problem, particularly as battlefield reverses became evident. Foreign Editor Ben Bassett cautioned us: "While continuing to tell the story as we see it, we can also be sure that we cover anything that might be considered positive or optimistic from the U.S. point of view. In other words don't be circumscribed in telling the story, but tell it fully." President Lyndon Baines Johnson was getting into the act, openly complaining about my and other AP reporting, and plotting to get me reassigned. I argued successfully that the public interest would best be served by reporting honest, accurate accounts of troops in action.

The controversy over coverage of the Vietnam war also began to put one generation of reporters against the other. There were those in the mainstream American media who did not like what we were doing and complained about our reporting wrecking a critically important American policy. They blamed our "insensitivity" on our inexperience. Joseph Alsop, the influential columnist, began calling us "young crusaders" and—along with other veterans of earlier wars such as Marguerite

Higgins and S.L.A. Marshall—demanded that we get off our high horses and get on the team.

By 1967 several hundred journalists were working out of Saigon, covering an increasingly brutal war, some of them depending to a considerable degree on "the five o'clock follies," the daily military briefing stage-managed by the senior information official, Barry Zorthian, popular with many journalists for his skills at propaganda—and poker. His main preoccupation was with positive stories. He would advise newly arrived officials, "Tell the truth, but don't blurt out everything you know." But Zorthian's media manipulation began to slip later in the year when the real cost of committing half a million men to Vietnam became impossible to conceal. Westmoreland's search-and-destroy strategy was becoming implausible, and the bloodshed and brutality that accompanied the troops into action was difficult to justify.

We were hearing reports that even Robert McNamara, the secretary of defense, was losing his enthusiasm for the war and was refusing to implement a request from Saigon for another increase in troops—an increase urgently needed because it was becoming clear that the war was bogging down in a stalemate. But Westmoreland put on a brave face, visited the United States in November 1967 and told anyone who would listen that the war was almost won. Meanwhile, a hundred other reporters and I covered the battle of Dak To, where one 173rd Airborne Brigade battalion lost more than 200 men in an afternoon.

The Tet Offensive came to Saigon and the rest of the country in January 1968, and the near total surprise of the dozens of Viet Cong attacks shook Vietnam—and the press corps—to their foundations. The war was suddenly outside the door of every journalist in town, and the reporting reflected the shock of discovery that no one anywhere was safe. The military high command, basing its assessment on kill statistics, tried to claim that the Tet attacks were a disaster for the Viet Cong and a victory for the United States. But even Robert McNamara knew the statistics lied; he'd already quit his job. So did President Lyndon Baines Johnson, who declined to seek another term in office.

And there was a time bomb ticking away at Tet that some officials in the military succeeded in concealing for a year or so, barbarous events at a place called My Lai involving American troops in a savage atrocity, events that when revealed to a stunned American public by reporter Sy Hersh destroyed whatever little support for the war remained.

But all that was 30 years ago. You're now at Robert's Field, Liberia, talking with a young American officer who has just told you he's neutral about the media, "It can help you, but it can also hurt you," his glance indicating he expects the second eventuality more likely than the first.

Vietnam was the excuse the Pentagon used to justify excessive media management in military actions against Grenada, Panama and Saddam Hussein's Iraq. There are signs that just maybe the military might be more considerate of media needs in future conflicts.

In the meantime, how do you convince a young American soldier in Liberia risking his life for his country that the story he's been hearing about the media ever since he joined the service—that we sold the military down the river in Vietnam, that we were destructive and not supportive—is just a part of the wider tragedy of that war? How do you convince him that a lot reporters cared so deeply about getting the story right that they followed troops into combat and died? And how do you convince him that the best interests of the military and the public are served by honest, accurate reporting about American troops in action—whether in the Central Highlands of Vietnam or the jungle of Liberia?

Peter Arnett, an international correspondent for CNN, covered the Vietnam War for the Associated Press.

Part IV
The 1970s

6

Ruben Salazar—Misunderstood Martyr

Frank del Olmo

Partly it was the way Ruben Salazar died. His head was shattered by a bullet-shaped tear-gas projectile fired by a deputy sheriff during a major riot in East Los Angeles in August 1970. Ever since, his death has been a sensitive subject for his colleagues and friends.

Ruben was on the job that day as *Los Angeles Times* columnist and news director for Los Angeles television station KMEX, and we can all envision ourselves the victim of the quirk of fate that found him in the wrong place at the wrong time.

But in the aftermath of his death, something else happened that made many journalists who knew Ruben uncomfortable. To the Mexican-American community whose problems he had written about, and to the Chicano activists whose protests he had covered, Salazar became a martyr. And that aura has grown with the passage of time. Parks, community centers and schools have been named after Salazar throughout the Southwest. There are even murals and Chicano posters that bear his likeness.

There is one artwork in particular, a silk screen by the famous Mexican muralist David Alfaro Siqueiros, that I'm uncomfortable looking at to this day. The likeness of Salazar that Siqueiros painted is almost saintlike, with a distant, long-suffering look to the eyes. It is not the earthy man I knew. He was an easygoing fellow who often jokingly lapsed into barrio slang—what we Latinos call Spanglish—when talking with friends. And, like many other reporters in those days, he sometimes drank a little more than he should have.

The canonization of Salazar unfortunately obscured not just the reality of his life but also the significance of his work. Salazar was, above all else, a pro. He was also, in his time, a unique and groundbreaking journalist who tried to work both for a mainstream newspaper and for a television station that served the Latino community. It wasn't easy, especially in the late 1960s when political passions in this country were running so high.

"A man in the middle" is how a black friend of Salazar's, William J. Drummond, once described him. "He was neither a pimp for the revolution nor a shill for the Establishment," Drummond wrote in Esquire. More than 25 years after his death, the genuine courage it took for Salazar to maintain that position, and the value it gave his journalism, is clearer than ever. So if there was a defining moment for American journalism in Salazar's life, it was most likely his decision, in early 1970, to be both a columnist for the *Times* and news director at KMEX.

A native of Ciudad Juárez, Mexico, Salazar was raised just across the border in El Paso, Texas, and became a naturalized U.S. citizen. Like many Chicanos in El Paso, his family lived a comfortable life compared to Mexicans on the other bank of the Rio Grande. After graduating from El Paso High School he served a two-year stint in the Army, then returned home to become one of the first Mexican Americans to study journalism at Texas Western College (now the University of Texas, El Paso.)

His first reporting job was at the *El Paso Herald-Post*, where he was the first Mexican American hired by that newspaper. His early work was guided by an editor, Ed Pooley, who was a champion of the city's Mexican-American community. Salazar covered both the police beat and Juárez, coming up with several exclusives, including a first-person account of horrific conditions in the El Paso jail. At least one former colleague of Salazar's, Earl Shorris, claims it was the first investigative piece ever done by an El Paso newspaper, and it helped change journalism in that city. "Ruben was the best reporter El Paso has ever seen," Shorris told Salazar's biographer, Mario T. Garcia.

So when Salazar moved to California in 1957, he was a seasoned reporter. He worked for the *Santa Rosa Press-Democrat* and *San Francisco News* before heading south to Los Angeles, working first at the Hearst-owned *Herald-Express* and then joining the *Los Angeles Times* in 1959. He wrote a prize-winning series for the *Times* on Mexican border issues and occasionally covered the local Mexican-American community, although, according to colleagues, he took pains to avoid being labeled the "Mexican reporter."

In 1965, Salazar was loaned by the city staff to the *Times'* foreign desk to cover the U.S. military intervention in the Dominican Republic. He so enjoyed being a foreign correspondent that he went abroad for three years, reporting from Vietnam and later manning the *Times'* Mexico City bureau.

He was called back to Los Angeles in 1968, according to his editors, because the city's large Mexican-American community was stirring with a more militant activism than Salazar had sometimes written about in the early part of the decade. That year a series of student strikes at several Latino high schools on the city's east side marked the emergence of a generation of young Latino activists who proudly called themselves Chicanos, a slang word for Mexican Americans.

The "East L.A. blowouts," as the student strikes came to be called, were followed in short order by Chicano protests aimed at the city's Board of Education, police department and even the local Roman Catholic church.

But despite his journalistic immersion in the militant protests of Los Angeles' Latino community, by 1970 Salazar did not fit any stereotypes of the "typical" Mexican American. He was married to an Anglo woman and lived a comfortably middle-class life, complete with a swimming pool, in suburban Orange County. So the journalists who worked with Salazar thought of him as a reporter first, a Mexican American second. And they were genuinely surprised at the outpouring of rage and grief in the Latino community that followed his death.

I can understand my colleagues' uneasiness at the heroic image many Latinos have of Ruben. But they might find it easier to comprehend if they remembered a couple of things about Salazar and the community that took him as its misunderstood martyr, in spite of himself.

The *Times* tried to cover the newly militant Latino community as thoroughly as it could. But much of what it published seemed dry and dispassionate compared to the anger and frustration being expressed on the streets. That is why Salazar's column drew so much attention when it first began to be published in 1970. For he seemed to be taking not just his own journalism but that of the *Times* to a new level that matched the passion being expressed on the city's streets.

One of Salazar's earliest columns, published on April 17, 1970, summarized the anger many Mexican Americans felt as bluntly as anything the *Times* had ever published: "...the word Mexican has been dragged through the mud of racism since the Anglos arrived in the Southwest," he wrote. "All this, and more, has contributed to the psychological crippling of the Mexican American when it comes to the word Mexican. He is unconsciously ashamed of it."

Such strong writing was made all the more powerful by the fact that Salazar was not just one of the few Mexican Americans working in journalism, but the only columnist.

He was 42 in 1970 and facing the normal challenges everyone does upon reaching middle age. But Salazar's mid-life crisis, if that's what it was, coincided with a time of remarkable ferment in the Mexican-American community.

Salazar left his reporting job at the *Times* in January 1970, after 11 years on the staff, to become news director at the city's first Spanish-language TV outlet, KMEX, the flagship station of what later evolved into the Univision network. There Salazar was enjoying the independence and authority his new job gave him. He told me once that, for the first time in his career, he felt he was talking to his own people instead of trying to explain Mexican Americans to others.

Working at KMEX reminded Salazar that, despite the growing militancy of the middle-class Mexican Americans and the young Chicanos whose protests he covered, the vast majority of Mexicans in Los Angeles were not nearly so radical. Thus, while Salazar saw his work at the *Times* as important, as helping shape public opinion, he saw his work at KMEX as even more fundamental. He wanted it to help educate and inform a large segment of the community that was still trapped in poor living and working conditions, and facing severe discrimination because it lacked political representation, education and economic power.

His new job also gave him the opportunity to immerse himself in the ferment that in those days had Latino barrios in such cultural and intellectual flux. As with the rest of American society, there had been activism in the barrios before but never on the scale of the late 1960s.

In response to the upheaval in the barrios, the *Times* gave Ruben an opportunity to write a weekly column about Chicano affairs after he left the regular staff. Even Ruben's friends were often unsettled by the angry tone he sometimes used writing about barrio problems. He didn't mince words when he discussed Anglo racism, but he never hesitated to criticize Mexican Americans when our shortcomings were to blame. For example, in a column about the difficulties that Latino civil-rights activists have had forming coalitions with their African-American counterparts, Salazar candidly wrote that part of the problem was that even Chicanos were "not untouched by bigotry."

While tragic, it is, in retrospect, fitting that Salazar died working as a journalist on a day of traumatic events. The Chicano protest he covered that hot, smoggy Saturday was the largest Mexican-American demonstration yet held in this country. It was a protest against the Vietnam War, in which Latino soldiers were dying in disproportionate numbers. In Los Angeles, that demonstration had been preceded by two years of militant Chicano protests against various social problems and injustices, like poor education, high unemployment and police brutality.

Throughout the rest of the Southwest, other Chicano groups had been springing up with similar protests, so that when more than 20,000 people gathered that Aug. 29, 1970, it was the high point of a movement that had been building for some time. People came from throughout the country to march down Whittier Boulevard, the busiest shopping street in the biggest barrio in the Southwest. There was a fiesta atmosphere to the event. Many people even brought their families.

After a three-mile-long march, the demonstrators arrived at Laguna Park (since renamed Salazar Park). There an anti-war rally began. Trouble started when Los Angeles County Sheriff's deputies, responding to reports of looting at a liquor store near the park, were pelted with rocks and bottles thrown from the fringes of the large crowd. A skirmish line of riot-equipped officers moved in to clear the park. A barrage of tear gas followed. Many protestors fled, some stayed and fought, and others headed back down Whittier Boulevard, taking out their anger on the businesses along the way.

For Los Angeles, it was the biggest, bloodiest riot since Watts had exploded five years earlier. Millions of dollars worth of property was destroyed, dozens of people were injured and arrested, and three people died, including Ruben Salazar. The Latino community would have mourned the victims no matter who they were, but the fact Salazar was among the dead seemed to compound the tragedy.

He was in the middle of the riot with a KMEX film crew. Walking along Whittier Boulevard, they went into a bar called the Silver Dollar Cafe to refresh themselves. Sheriff's deputies arrived a few minutes later, responding to reports that a man with a rifle had entered the bar. One deputy herded people standing in the doorway back inside. A second fired tear gas into the room. Instead of using a canister that he could have rolled underneath a curtain that covered the door, the second deputy fired a tear-gas projectile that ripped through the air like a small missile. It tore through the curtain and hit Salazar in the head.

As the injured newsman slumped to the floor, the other bar patrons, including Salazar's film crew, fled out the back. Some told deputies that an injured man lay inside, but officers did not enter the building for hours, long after Salazar was dead.

Why the deputies acted as they did, from the start of the incident to the end, has never been adequately answered. And it has fed conspiracy theories that grew up around the slaying of Salazar. Unfortunately, the cold, arrogant manner in which Los Angeles County authorities handled the matter only fed the suspicions of Chicano activists.

The only official inquiry into the Salazar killing was a coroner's inquest that could legally answer only one question: Had Salazar died "at the hands of another"? The inquest concluded that he had, yet not one of the deputies involved was ever put on trial. Ultimately, a wrongful death lawsuit filed by Salazar's widow was settled out of court, an inconclusive and unsatisfying end to what had been a traumatic experience for Los Angeles' Latino community.

Most of the activists who mourned Salazar did not know him, but they knew of him. His reporting did not cater to them. A few of them even considered him a sellout *Tio Taco*. But they knew he paid attention to them. As a young journalist just out of college, I could move a bit more freely among young Chicano militants than the widely recognized Salazar could. And on many occasions I heard his columns, which left Anglo readers so unsettled, criticized by Chicanos for not being militant *enough*.

Thus I found it ironic, and even a bit hypocritical, to later see some of those same Chicano militants shedding tears at Salazar's funeral. But perhaps I judged them too harshly, given my own youthful idealism at the time. Maybe they came to understand just how much the Latino community had lost after Salazar was gone. Certainly few of them could have written columns explaining the appeal to barrio youngsters of militant Chicano groups like the Brown Berets (who modeled themselves after the Black Panther Party) and get such columns published in the *Los Angeles Times*.

To this day many Latino activists believe Salazar's death was not accidental. They will always be sure that his death was an assassination carried out by dark, sinister forces fearful of the influence and power Salazar had as a columnist and news executive. While I do not subscribe to those theories, I do know that Salazar's death was a devastating loss to a community that was just starting to find its voice. The emotions Salazar's death stirred are not surprising.

Another thing Salazar's former colleagues forget is that he was changing during the last few months of his life. Only once do I remember hearing an Anglo friend of Salazar say he thought the man was changing, maybe even finding himself, in his new role. With a quarter century of hindsight, I now realize that is exactly what was happening.

I remember the last conversation I had with him, the day before he died. The Chicano anti-war march was already looming as the biggest

Latino protest ever. "We have really been covering it here," he said, referring to KMEX newscast. "I hope the *gente* [people] really turn out for it. We have to show the Anglo what we can do."

I'm not suggesting Salazar had become an activist Chicano, but he was certainly not the same man he was when he left the *Times*. In his private life, Ruben was going through the same turmoil many Latinos were dealing with in those days. Like a relative handful of successful Mexican Americans, Salazar had made it in the Anglo world. But by the '60s another generation had come along, inspired by the civil-rights movement and Cesar Chavez's campaign to unionize farm workers. They questioned the assimilationist path that Ruben and others like him had taken. And they did not raise these questions quietly. They protested and demonstrated on a scale their elders had never attempted.

Impelled by his professional responsibility, Salazar reported on this phenomenon. But it affected him. He was disciplined enough to report on it accurately and fairly but human enough to ponder the hard questions these young militants were asking.

I think he often wrote his columns explaining things like, Who is a Chicano? and What is it that Chicanos want? as much to clarify things in his own mind as he did to clarify them for his readers. And one of the saddest things about Salazar's death is that he died never having fully answered many of those questions for himself, or for the Mexican-American community.

Still, one of Salazar's legacies to American journalism is that he proved a journalist can be both an able professional and a sensitive chronicler of a unique community. At a time when journalists of various ethnicities, as well as women and gay reporters, face similar challenges, Salazar can stand as a role model for all of them. Even if he was unable to answer all the questions his journalism raised, his striving to do so was both honorable and inspirational.

In the end, neither Salazar's journalistic colleagues nor his Chicano admirers, and I include myself in both groups, fully knew the man who died that fiery Aug. 29. I know he was not a Chicano saint. But I also know he was not just another Mexican American.

What Ruben Salazar was, and what he might have become, will never be fully known. And while that is not the greatest tragedy of the East Los Angeles riot, it remains, for me, the most profound.

Frank del Olmo is assistant to the editor of the Los Angeles Times *and a regular columnist.*

7

Past and Present at Wounded Knee

Robert Allen Warrior

In the early morning hours of Feb. 28, 1973, 200 Lakota people and their supporters from the American Indian Movement (AIM) seized the hamlet of Wounded Knee, S.D. in a desperate, last-ditch effort to draw attention to dire conditions on the Pine Ridge Sioux Reservation. Within moments of arriving at Wounded Knee, the reservation residents and militant activists ransacked a trading post, took possession of a church and held a dozen hostages at gunpoint.

The hostages were soon released, but the takeover lasted 71 days and drew unprecedented attention to the contemporary situation of Native American people and communities. Although Wounded Knee climaxed a series of actions by American Indian activists—including the 19-month occupation of Alcatraz Island that began in November of 1969 and the takeover of the Bureau of Indian Affairs (BIA) building during election week of 1972—it was really the first moment to which the press devoted sustained attention to Native issues.

As Paul Chaat Smith (a Washington, D.C.-based Comanche writer) and I were doing the research for our book about those years in Indian country (and I don't mean Vietnam), I was struck on numerous occasions by the way Wounded Knee could be a starting point for so many people.

One of the first lessons journalists learned at Wounded Knee, and they came in droves from around the world, was that they were arriving very late to a story that had deserved their attention much earlier. In spite of that, they did their collective job fairly well. Reporters from the mainstream press pieced together the puzzle and, having looked at their efforts with the benefit of hindsight and lots of information not available to them then, their work still fits together pretty well. Radical journalists (we all remember them, right?) formed a collective and managed to get a lot of good information out to their constituencies.

That journalists mostly did their job and did it well is no surprise, given that Wounded Knee occurred in an era when journalists doing their jobs well brought down a president and became a force for societal change. Their good work, though, is surprising given the challenges they faced. Competing government agencies couldn't get their stories straight or even their chain of command worked out. Moreover, the events at Wounded Knee pitted a duly elected (but despotic) tribal official against a group of his own citizens. At least four different groups set up armed bunkers and roadblocks.

Not to mention the bullets, tens of thousands of which were flying during the takeover. Two people inside Wounded Knee died. One federal agent was permanently paralyzed from the waist down. Many other people were wounded. Most people there for some of the more dramatic firefights were amazed that there weren't more casualties.

I have looked at a lot of footage of tracers in the South Dakota sky; I have heard audiotapes from bunkers that recorded the fear in the voices of those who manned them during firefights; and I have seen pictures of the blood-soaked wounded. I believe war correspondents who say that covering battles is the most hair-raising reporting one can do. And there was something very much like a battle going on at Wounded Knee.

The guns were why so many journalists were there. The armored personnel carriers that surrounded Wounded Knee were why, even towards the end, when the whole thing was not much more than a terrible mess, journalists remained as chroniclers and witnesses.

Participants in earlier actions by Native activists typically don't remember it this way, but the story of the incredible changes taking place in the Indian world during the 1970s was barely on the public agenda before Wounded Knee. The Alcatraz occupation garnered much local Bay Area coverage, but in that 19-month period, the three networks carried a total of only four stories on their national evening news broadcasts. The takeover of the BIA headquarters during election week of 1972 could have easily ended cataclysmically. Explosives deployed by the militants inside could have easily made the granite building a pile of rubble resting on top of perhaps 1,000 dead Native bodies. Yet outside of Washington, hardly any print or broadcast media paid much attention.

Less spectacular developments—new policy and education initiatives, educational and professional advancement—were buried where few readers would notice. Then, as now, ongoing developments in the prospects of Native people and communities just aren't interesting to very many people. Editors wanting to include coverage of Native American issues face the very real problem of needing to have stories their readers will read. And Native Americans are a tiny group of about 2 million.

Those editors could make the somewhat valid argument that American society includes dozens of ethnic groups that are larger than Native Americans who also face problems in trying to establish themselves economically, socially and culturally. But that isn't enough. In many ways, Native Americans are unique. A bureau of the U.S. government is responsible for their affairs. Federal officials are appointed by the president to look after their prospects. They have nation-to-nation relationships with the United States that have been upheld in various ways by the Supreme Court since the 1830s and supported by every presidential administration for the past six decades except Eisenhower's.

Wounded Knee taught the press those things, if only for a time. And journalists informed viewers and readers. A Harris poll done over a month into the 71-day takeover showed that 93 percent of Americans were aware of and were following what happened at Wounded Knee (that might be a higher percentage that can correctly name the current president of the United States). Fifty-one percent of those people were sympathetic to the Native people inside. Only 21 percent were opposed.

Part of what made wounded knee so compelling was the setting: In 1890, it was the scene of a massacre of 200 Native Americans at the hands of U.S. military forces. At Alcatraz, federal negotiators had worried that they would have another Wounded Knee on their hands. In Washington in 1972, those same negotiators said they were attempting to avoid another Wounded Knee. Suddenly, in the winter of 1973, they had to worry over avoiding another Wounded Knee at Wounded Knee.

Reporters who arrived there found an action in which local, reservation-based people had invited the mostly urban-based militants of AIM to join them in drawing attention to the repressive policies and practices of a despotic tribal leader, Dick Wilson, who was conducting what some deemed a "reign of terror" against his own people.

For once, Native American people had the full benefit of journalism at their disposal. Well-informed reporters could help promote understanding of tough issues. Business journals ran articles about specific labor problems facing reservation people, one of which carried the headline "Payrolls: An Answer to the Indian Militants." Long feature stories in major magazines made sense of the contemporary Indian story in a way not done before. Wounded Knee was a fixture on the national evening news for weeks; although stories tended to be short and focused on people shooting at each other, some of the reporting was quite informed, fair and balanced.

Certainly not all the press was kind, generous and fair. Some people revealed some seriously offensive ignorance along the way. Terri Schultz, in an article called "Bamboozle Me Not at Wounded Knee" for *Harper's*, seemed as green as they come in allowing her expectations and preconceived stereotypes to guide her through her story. Her worst moment, in which she was joined by some other writers reporting the same event, was when she dwelt at length on an incident involving Indian people not knowing how to butcher a head of cattle that some of the occupiers had rustled up. This lack of knowledge was, to her, clear proof that these people were anything but Indians. Forget that they were, at best, 100 years distant from their ancestors who hunted bison. Indeed, many of the AIM activists had earned their considerable rage growing up impoverished and ignored in cities, often so poor that nearly all their food was in the form of government commodities (let them eat cheese!). Schultz knew enough about Indians to know that these folks at Wounded Knee were not who they purported to be.

But compared to the relatively scant Alcatraz coverage—in which terms like "squaw," "brave" and even "heap big" showed up with alarming frequency—the professional journalists who covered Wounded Knee learned a lot and learned it quick. The event was big enough, in fact, to have prompted sincere debate about whether or not the press had played its proper role in its coverage. As Desmond Smith opined in *The Nation*:

> ...Wounded Knee was an example of a new and expanding strategy of political manipulation that neatly circumvents the ordinary processes of government. Its essential element is that it makes a direct and powerful appeal to the public through the mass media.... It is now entirely possible for a small group of people to intimidate the strongest of governments. It is quite clear from this that such individuals can seize upon a real political grievance, stage it imaginatively, bring in the media, and proceed that their own particular solution must be accepted by everybody else.

Harper's and *National Review* published articles that by and large agreed with Smith.

But others reminded their peers that prior to the taking of Wounded Knee, the press was nowhere to be found. The people of Pine Ridge, along with Native people in other places, were suffering. Like any modern people facing modern problems, they often need the press as a court of last resort, a conduit for information under extreme circumstances. The reservation people who took Wounded Knee were not freewheeling college students or crazed militants. They were a desperate, vulnerable people suffering at the hands of their own U.S. taxpayer-supported tribal government. The U.S. government was doing nothing for them. National Indian organizations offered no help. They had nowhere else to turn but to a ragtag group of militants who believed in going anywhere to stand with Indian people. And when together they provoked a military response from the United States and bullets started flying, all of those people who before were unable and unwilling to help them arrived—including the national press.

Hank Adams, an Assiniboine-Sioux veteran of Indian affairs who acted as an intermediary at Wounded Knee, argued before Congress that the Fourth Estate needed to continue doing its homework to become an instrument of recourse for Native people. As he said in that forum, "The role of the news media in bringing about a termination or prolongment of such actions as the Wounded Knee occupation—or the BIA building occupation—should become a matter of conscientious consideration by members of its professions."

Coverage of Native Americans has improved since Wounded Knee, but never again have so many reporters done so much to bring the benefits of their profession to Native American coverage. I certainly do not think every reporter should sink her or his teeth deeply into the topic of contemporary Indian affairs. I continue to think, though, that more news organizations would do a lot for coverage of Native issues generally by assigning at least a few reporters to keeping track of what's happening in the lives of Indian people and the agencies that so thoroughly impinge upon their lives. Covering Native America means being willing to sift through court documents, government reports and ancient subtexts. Arcane federal policy is central to the story.

Reading a few Native American newsweeklies, developing a few contacts among Native journalists (wonderful professionals who have excellent files and often a willingness to share what they know) or even attending the annual meeting of the Native American Journalists Association are not overly difficult things to add even to a hectic schedule. For those who like to gamble, going to a reservation that runs a casino can be a good way of combining business and pleasure.

Native Americans have a future, and journalists will play a role in reporting their possibilities. Do yourself a favor and do a little digging. It's a really good story.

Robert Allen Warrior (Osage), is a journalist and professor of English at Stanford University. His most recent book is Like a Hurricane; The Indian Movement from Alcatraz to Wounded Knee *(New Press, 1996), which he co-authored with Paul Chaat Smith.*

8

The Weight of Watergate

Ellen Hume

Twenty-five years after the Watergate break-in, American journalism is still recovering from its most celebrated triumph. Woodward and Bernstein bagged the big one—the president of the United States—in a David and Goliath drama that turned obscure reporters into pop-culture heroes.

Of course it wasn't really like that. Despite the heroics of Robert Redford and Dustin Hoffman in *All the Presidents Men*, the reality included not just an intrepid newspaper but, necessarily, the Congress and the courts. It was Vietnam as much as Watergate that sealed the cynicism of today's journalists. President Nixon's downfall wasn't really the starting point for today's "gotcha" journalism culture. As scholar James L. Aucoin has observed, there is plenty of evidence to indicate that 20 years before Watergate, "investigative journalism" was reappearing as an alternative to less trenchant forms of reporting.

And contrary to the popular myth, journalism schools were not inundated suddenly with fresh recruits to follow in the footsteps of Woodward and Bernstein. The surge in students working for journalism degrees began earlier, as Michael Schudson argues in *Watergate in American Memory*, at least in part because of the growth in the number of students pursuing advertising degrees within programs in journalism or communication. Outside of colleges and universities, the nation's press corps proliferated because of the public events of the 1960s, from the civil rights movement to the assassinations and Vietnam War protests. Moreover, the social and technological revolutions brought new opportunities for women in journalism, increased the salaries and class status of journalists, expanded the popularity of local television news programs and created all of the new news outlets, from the magazine shows to 24-hour news services on cable and the Internet.

Yet Watergate still stands out as one of the great turning points in American journalism. It remains the inspiration for a generation of reporters, a justification for journalistic intrusion and a paramount example of how the balance of power has shifted from the politicians to the news media.

During Watergate, reporters braved IRS audits, FBI wiretaps, threats from the attorney general and other abuses of government power as targets on President Nixon's enemies list. Today's Woodwards and Bernsteins aren't the lonely warriors anymore—they're Goliath. Journalists are seen increasingly as the ones who are abusing their own special constitutional privileges; they are being slapped by the courts for invading privacy with deceptive practices and have lost favor with the public they supposedly represent. During the Watergate era in 1972, 30 percent of the public had a great deal of confidence in the press and 41 percent in television news. Louis Harris' February 1997 poll, however, found that only 11 percent of the public had such confidence in the press, and 18 percent in television news.

To be sure, if the public's respect for the press has fallen since Watergate, it is not alone. Virtually every institution is seen now in a more negative light. Journalists are particularly vulnerable because they must ask painful questions no one else wants to face. Often they are tarred unfairly as the messengers of bad news. In a time of financial cutbacks, when government is no longer looked to for sweeping action, politics and journalism are driven by a demonizing process that focuses on moral issues. They don't cost anything.

Now, both government and media are seen as out of control and in need of ethical boundaries. Scholars Thomas Patterson and Kathleen Hall Jamieson argue that the obsessive negativity of today's scandal-seeking journalists has undermined not only the public's opinion of politicians, but of the press itself. It is hard to remember today the underdog courage of the *Washington Post*'s lonely Watergate coverage. Today virtually any rumor of a political scandal is picked up and mass marketed through the ubiquitous news and infotainment media, even if it comes from obviously tainted political origins. The power of the story is exaggerated by the sheer size and scope of today's press corps, whose appearance at an event brings down an avalanche of print reporters, television correspondents, producers, editors, engineers and assorted assistants. There were, for example, 15,000 people describing themselves as journalists registered at the Democratic National Convention in Chicago last summer, covering only 4,289 delegates who had no real job to do.

All of this is amplified by the unavoidable dominance now of the electronic media—television news in particular—in our sensory and political environments. Once simply a sideshow, television news is now the main source of political information for most Americans. As Howard Kurtz and James Fallows observed in their recent books decrying celebrity journalists, the television pundit business has virtually overtaken fact-finding. Audiences for national television news and most newspapers continue to drop alarmingly, thanks to ever-expanding competition from cable, the Internet, CD-ROMs, home video and other factors. In a panic to hold onto mass audiences that are slipping away, many news organizations are on a tabloid treadmill, looking for ever more sensational infotainments.

These journalists have largely squandered whatever moral authority they may have gained with Watergate. Too many are in the opinion, prediction, gossip and celebrity business, rather than in the business of presenting verified facts of relevance to citizens in a democracy.

The ranks of journalism have expanded to include all manner of television pundits, politicians and crackpots, and the emphasis on verification and balance has receded. It meant something when Edward R. Murrow or Walter Cronkite frowned on Sen. Joseph McCarthy or the Vietnam War; now there are simply too many "journalists" with too few threshold tests for what deserves to be "news."

Thus the content and process of news gathering have helped to corrode the public's trust. Today many investigative reporters come across as mercenaries for giant media conglomerates, searching out scandal stories not because they want to right wrongs, but because they want to sell them as entertainment. Media feeding frenzies such as the O.J. Simpson trials and the stakeout of Bill Cosby's home after his son Ennis' murder, together with such embarrassments as the faked NBC "Dateline" truck explosion and the designation of George Stephanopoulos and Pat Buchanan as television journalists, further erode the public's respect for today's genuine Woodwards and Bernsteins. The Roper Center's poll for *Parade* magazine, published March 2, 1997, found that more than half of the people polled felt the news was too biased, and a whopping 90 percent said the media's desire to make profits improperly influenced the news. In the popular culture, reporters are no longer depicted as Clark Kent, let alone Superman; instead they are often the bad guys. Even PBS's "Magic School Bus" science program for children casts the television journalist as a villain who creates a fake sea monster in order to get a big scoop.

The Watergate era wasn't quite the golden age of perfect reporting that some seem to remember. It was anonymous sources like Deep Throat that made the *Washington Post*'s Watergate coverage possible. Yet it was "the high mark in public confidence in the press as a democratic institution in American politics," according to Kenneth Dautrich of the Roper Center.

The now mythic legend of Watergate has reinforced a cynical self-righteousness, a Spanish Inquisitioner's zeal that is wholly inconsistent with the realities of history, politics or reporters' own lives. It is true that deceitful behavior of some officials in virtually every administration and Congress has justified the press corps' vigilance and skepticism. But now the worst motives are assumed, regardless of the facts.

"Vietnam together with Watergate destroyed whatever trust that generally existed between the press and the government, and now we are living with the gruesome consequences," concludes Marvin Kalb, director of Harvard's Joan Shorenstein Center on the Press, Politics and Public Policy. Journalists have elevated one scandal after another to "gate" status—from Iraqgate to Troopergate to Travelgate to Filegate—but none yet has reached the high Water mark. Even the Reagan administration's Iran-Contra scandal, during which White House officials asked Saudi Arabian officials and other foreign donors to help fund an illegal war in Nicaragua, did not sweep people out of office and into jail the way Watergate did.

Part of the reason is that the public didn't want another president to fail as Nixon did in Watergate. But part of it also is that for decades journalists have been asking the Watergate smoking-gun question— "What did the president know and when did he know it?"—instead of moving past this personal framework to investigate the patterns and practices that corrupt American democracy. Even though one of the main legacies of Watergate was the well-known advice to "follow the money," today's journalists have dallied far too long on personality defects and bedroom behavior. Journalists—and I include myself because I worked for the *Wall Street Journal* at the time—were slow to notice the regulatory changes that led to the savings and loan scandal and the creeping influence of soft money fund-raising schemes on governance at all levels.

While a fundraising scandal offers, in President Clinton's own handwriting, a plan to market the Lincoln Bedroom to his large campaign donors, the public is remarkably uninterested in the news. A Feb. 28, 1997, CNN-*Time* poll showed President Clinton's popularity at 60 percent, despite the fact that 53 percent said they felt his campaign finance behavior was unethical. The danger is that the watchdog, having barked at the wrong things, now has lost its bite.

Verdicts are going against the news media in more than just the case of Food Lion vs. Capital Cities/ABC, Inc. The media's rate of successful defenses (28.5 percent) in the 14 libel, privacy and related trials in 1996 was the lowest ever reported; the median award ($2.38 million) against news organizations was the highest, thanks to a surge in punitive damages, according to the Libel Defense Resource Center, which tracks such statistics. "In some of the recent cases, like Food Lion, with multimillion-dollar verdicts, people are simply reacting negatively to the press," concludes Laura Handman, a First Amendment lawyer who has represented *BusinessWeek* and other news organizations.

Ironically, the anti-media campaign that President Nixon hoped would save him in 1972 has now taken hold. The institution that helped to bring him down is now viewed, according to polls and focus groups, as another powerful special interest. When millionaire ABC journalist Sam Donaldson accepted government subsidies for his sheep ranch, it became that much more difficult to depict journalists as the public-spirited heroes of *All the Presidents Men.*

Unless journalists work effectively to earn back the public's trust, they may not be able to serve democracy effectively by exposing painful facts that the nation needs to face. With juries seemingly poised to punish the press for their intrusive powers, the media's own corporate lawyers may say it's not worth the risk to publish or broadcast controversial news. And even if they do get the facts, the public may not act because they have been numbed by the constant barrage of post-Watergate scandals.

Ellen Hume is executive director of PBS's Democracy Project and a panelist on CNN's "Reliable Sources." For 20 years she was a reporter for the Wall Street Journal, *the* Los Angeles Times *and other newspapers.*

9

Newspapers for Working People

Pete Hamill

When I first walked into a city room in the summer of 1960, I felt as if my life had finally begun. I had never been to journalism school. I hadn't even finished high school. But I was filled with that mixture of chutzpah and possibility that in those days filled so many children of immigrants. In the decade after the war, a gloriously optimistic period in New York, we believed we could do anything with our lives. We could be presidents of the United States. We could play left field for the Brooklyn Dodgers. We could even be newspapermen.

That invincible, adolescent optimism was not misplaced. It was the engine of millions of American careers, from law, medicine and the arts to the more raffish trade of the newspaper world. The wish was transformed into reality for many of us by one of the greatest pieces of social legislation of this century: the GI Bill of Rights. The Bill, as we all called it, meant that the children of bricklayers and laborers and machinists could enter those centers of higher education from which they had been barred by economics and class. And if very few of us were elected president and only a fortunate few played left field for the Dodgers, most of us realized lives that were beyond the imaginations of our parents.

My own erratic path took me to art schools, to Mexico, to literature and finally to the city room of Dorothy Schiff's *New York Post*. Once I joined the rowdy confraternity of newspaper people, I never wanted to do anything else.

In those days, when there were still seven daily newspapers in New York, there were copy editors who worked nights at the *Post* and days at the *Times* and never did pay off their bookmakers. There were still boomers around then, men of great talent who would arrive one evening at the rewrite desk, turn out brilliant copy for three or four months, and then abruptly come in drunk, heave a typewriter out a window and move on. Sometimes they moved up the block to the *World-Telegram and Sun*, or the *Journal American*; often they drifted out to Columbus or St. Louis or the edge of the Pacific. Wives would come looking for them; children would call the city desk; but they were gone. A few wrote novels. Some became screenwriters. Most simply vanished.

Those who stayed were a hard, tough, often cynical lot, filled with savage humor and the wisdom of the streets that gave them life. They had started out in the Depression, or had learned the trade at *Stars and Stripes* or had risen through the ranks from the worn bench where generations of copy boys had cased the room. Many were the children of immigrants, or products of the GI Bill.

There was almost no talk about such high falutin' notions as ethnicity on the *Post*. Most of the reporters, photographers and editors came from the mainstream of the European immigration wave; they were the children of the Irish, the Italians and Eastern European Jews who had crossed continents and oceans to get to New York. But there were WASPs among them, and women and a few African Americans. In general, issues of class, race or ethnicity were less important than issues of craft. The *Post* was liberal in its politics and covered the civil rights movement in the South and continued to have a beat reporter on the union movement. But I don't remember any feeling in the city room that we were all engaged in a crusade.

The newspapermen I knew were all the children of working-class Americans. They were delighted to be in the newspaper trade, because they knew what it meant to break up sidewalks for a living or work in sewers or run into burning buildings as firemen. They knew such things because those were the jobs their fathers did. Their street reporting was informed by the special knowledge that came from growing up on those streets. If they encountered a plumber or a longshoreman, they knew the language, understood the nuances of most talk and could fit minor tragedies or large disasters into a wider urban context.

They knew that they would never get rich in the newspaper business, but their hands would be clean at the end of the shift. And almost always, the checks cleared. I still possess a pay stub from those years, showing that I had earned $109 that week, including night differential. In all the years since then, I've never felt richer.

It is not, of course, news to say that everything has changed. There are three major daily newspapers in New York City now. There are no more boomers. There are no gray-faced rewritemen smoking Camels as they type. There are no typewriters, either (although I keep one at home to use during power blackouts and other acts of the Newspaper God). Even the newspaper saloon is gone, the marvelous—and dangerous—institution that served as postgraduate school and hiring hall for thousands of men and women.

Like most important changes, social or cultural, there was no defining date for this change. It happened while too many other things were happening; a reporter was sent to Saigon or Mississippi, and when he came back there was a copy boy in the room with a degree from Harvard. By the late 1970s, such changes were no longer remarkable.

I don't mean to lament completely what has been lost. Newspapers today are more professional than they have ever been. Reporters are better educated, and although the hiring of women and minorities remains imperfect, it is infinitely better in most places than it was when I was young. Ethical standards are also more rigid—the old cozy relationships among reporters, cops and politicians have been drastically altered and this is a gain for the readers.

But there have been other alterations that might not be as healthy. When I became a newspaperman, my father was still working in a factory, wiring fluorescent lamps. My mother was working as a cashier in a movie house. Those of my friends who didn't use the GI Bill became cops and firemen. Our families remained as densely meshed as the neighborhood did; I am still in touch with people who were with me in grammar school. Their views of the world, shaped by the ethos of blue-collar America, remained a constant in my own mind as I went about my duties as a newspaperman. I wanted to know how people made a living, how they fed their children, paid their rent, bought clothes. I knew what a humiliation it was for a father to lose a job because my own father had once lost his.

As industrial jobs began to vanish and unions started to shrink and the welfare rolls exploded, the subject matter of newspapers was altered. Murder became routine. Old working-class neighborhoods fell into deep decay. I covered such stories with a natural empathy; these people were not statistics in a sociology textbook. They were like the people I knew as a boy. As a newspaperman covering this complicated story, I was not alone in my empathy. Almost everybody I worked with in the early '60s was one generation away from manual labor, or poverty.

That too has changed. The underpaid and overworked newspaper people of my youth were city people. Some of them were bohemians, some were rowdies, some were drunks; most of them were terrible husbands and inconstant wives. But they were something to see at a murder scene or typing with two fingers on deadline or correcting barbarisms in copy. And Jesus, they were fun.

The newspaper life was changed by a number of factors. Careerists began to dominate craftsmen in all areas of American life; it wasn't enough to carve leather into a perfect shoe; you must also long to run the shoe company. More important, the Newspaper Guild did an honorable job of getting publishers to pay newspaper people what they were worth. That is, they moved them into the middle class. Soon reporters, rewritemen, editors and photographers began doing what many city-born middle-class Americans did: They moved to the suburbs. An urban trade was soon being practiced by suburbanites. This was a huge change. It was inconceivable to my generation that you would hurry off to catch the 6:22 to the suburbs, or invite your friends to backyard barbecues, or have two cars, a stable marriage and investments in mutual funds. When I was young, I never heard a newspaperman mention the word pension; we were too busy getting out tomorrow's paper. And when the paper was locked up, we hurried off to a saloon.

The change wasn't only a shift into the middle class. For perfectly decent and honorable reasons, laws were passed to bring some equality to the process of hiring Americans. For too long a time, blacks, Latinos and women had been frozen out of many areas of employment, from law firms to newspapers. The law was clear; the system must be opened up to all; the promises made by America must be kept.

But there was a down side. It was no longer possible for an editor to look at a kid with talent and say, "Give this guy a shot." Papers must first be filled out. Educational accomplishments must be listed. For the first time, personnel managers and human relations experts became part of the process of hiring newspaper people. How could an editor justify hiring a high school dropout over someone with an M.A.? If you had a hot raw talent from a community college, how could he or she get a chance before someone with a degree from Stanford?

Staffs of newspapers began to be layered with young people who had basic skills but no passion; their resumes were often better than their reportorial skills; they found little joy in climbing fire escapes at three in the morning to interview the grieving mother of the dead gang leader. I suspect that many of them were the children of the men who had moved away from blue-collar America through the GI Bill. They were serious; they were well-schooled; but too often, they were separated by their parents' success from the people whose lives they were being asked to chronicle. They could even explain a 401K.

I realize here that I'm in danger of falling into the marsh of nostalgia, mistaking my own golden youth for a lost golden age. I hope not. But I am now a proud member of a craft that today would not grant me entry. There is no room in my trade anymore for high school dropouts, or for people without university degrees. That is to say, the city room is no longer open to the likes of Damon Runyon, Jimmy Breslin or Ernest Hemingway.

Still, a part of me remains infused with the incurable optimism of my generation. New York today is like many other American cities: caught up in the largest immigration wave since the turn of the last century. The new immigrants began arriving in the late 1970s, parts of small streams that began to merge into mighty rivers. They were following upon another huge demographic shift: the exodus of millions of whites to the suburbs and the simultaneous arrival in Northern cities of millions of blacks and Puerto Ricans. These migrants were American citizens, but unlike the earlier European immigrants, their timing was dreadful. They arrived in the Northern cities at the same time that American industry was closing the factories that had supported my father and millions like him. The lack of jobs for badly educated people was a guarantee of calamity, and for a long time newspapers were often filled with examples of that calamity. This time, it was not taking place in some distant place. It was happening in neighborhoods where many of us on newspapers had grown up. The distinctions between class, race and ethnicity began to blur. Too often, "black" and "Latino" were used as synonyms for "poor."

At first, reporters used conventional tools to chronicle these shifts. They went to murders or riots or fires and wrote down the names and ages of the dead and injured. This was not enough. Often they found that the old skills were inadequate, that the assumptions of the children of white immigrants were not always the same as those of African or Latino Americans. The myths were different. The psychological templates were cut in apparently different ways. It seemed that blacks and Latinos didn't see the city as a place of hope or opportunity. Reporters needed new tools, new ways to make contact with the subjects of our inquiries.

Newspapers at last started hiring black and Latino reporters. Editors learned to step back and think more deeply and broadly about what their reporters were covering. They began to acknowledge cities. If too many newspaper people surrendered to glib despair, others—not all of them black or Latino—wrote about the heroic struggles of many people to rise above the wider calamity.

The experience of covering American migrants has helped us to deal with the great wave of new immigrants. Remembering the way we often floundered in covering Americans who were new to cities has helped us to see the city through the eyes of strangers. I would dishonor the sacrifices and pain of my own parents if I did not try to make my own newspaper into an institution of welcome and celebration for those immigrants. This is personal, of course; it is not an attitude that rises from the abstractions of sociology. I see a Jamaican woman emptying bedpans in a hospital and I see my mother, who once did the same job. I see a Mexican man heaving garbage cans into a truck outside a restaurant, and I see my father. I see Koreans and Pakistanis and Russians and Dominicans doing the lousiest jobs in my city, and I see the Irish, the Italians and the Jews. As a newspaperman who is also a son of immigrants, I must keep one thing in mind: They are us.

And in order to know their stories, in order to explain New York to the immigrants and the immigrants to New York, I must have reporters who can speak their languages. I have a Korean reporter out in the newsroom now. I have a woman reporter who was born in Russia and another from Santo Domingo. More are coming. I will never hire someone to fill a quota. But no big city newspaper can do the job properly these days if the reporters are standing tongue-tied at a crime scene or are unable to understand the lyrics of the new love songs or read the nuances of life among the new immigrants and their children. If a reporter sees an immigrant as the Other, the reporter will fail in the basic task of reporting: to see. There is a great, splendid, American story happening all around us, and we must have the tools to cover it. One essential tool is language.

The arrival among us of the children of the new immigrants, combined with the enormous successes of African Americans, is a wonderful moment for the country, the culmination of a difficult, often desperate century. It is also at the heart of my optimism about the craft of newspapering and the continuing vitality of American newspapers. My father and mother became Americans by reading newspapers. If we do our work well, so will the new immigrants. It will be a long time before we see an immigrant whip out a laptop on the subway to read the latest news. Newspapers must do for the new immigrants what newspapers did for the European immigrants of the past. We must help them to become Americans.

There is an added benefit: If newspapers truly begin to reflect the dynamism of American cities, if they cover the city that *is* instead of the city that *was*, the craft will flourish. Typewriters will not return. The sound of the AP ticker will not hammer through city rooms. But we will find for ourselves a passionate new generation of talented city people whose presence will enrich us. The children of immigrants discover America every day, for themselves, for their parents, for us. These new reporters, covering this huge new story, will reinvigorate the staffs of every American newspaper while replenishing our audiences. They will help alter the language, the way Yiddish-speaking reporters once did, as did those who grew up with the language of the blues. In search of the news, they will give us fresher myths and alternate narratives. They will help us to see the new world that they are helping to create, the world of the 21st century.

Perhaps most important, they will help bring newspapers closer to the people who need them. The children of the new immigrants are closer to working people than most of us are, because their mothers have worked in sweat shops, their fathers have worked 14-hour days in grocery stores, their parents have emptied bedpans and garbage cans so that their children would never have to do that work. They are children of sacrifice and hope. We are fools if we don't hand them the most precious document I've ever held in my hand: a press card.

Pete Hamill, a reporter and author, began his writing career at the New York Post *in 1960. He is former editor in chief of the New York* Daily News.

Part V
The 1980s

10

We've Come a Long Way—Maybe

Koky Dishon

New York cafe singer Bobby Short was going home—home to Danville, Ill.—to be celebrated and to entertain at the community's 12-year-old symphony orchestra's first sold-out performance.

Charles Leroux, a writer with the *Chicago Tribune*'s Tempo section, made the journey with Short and returned to share an American experience with all its paradoxes. It was April 2, 1980.

"Like a necklace of shining jewels curved to the bosom of the Vermilion River where its banks widen to form Lake Vermilion, the procession of car lights in the rainy night stretched down from town, across the bridge, and up to the country club above the far shore," Leroux wrote. "'John O'Hara,' Bobby Short said, 'would have loved it.' Yes, he would have loved the irony of the motorcade filing to a reception honoring the little black boy from the North End of the city who had grown up to become the troubadour of Manhattan cafe society.... And he'd have noted the moment when Short turned from the greeters and huggers and autograph seekers and said, 'I never learned to swim properly. I wasn't allowed in the YMCA pool.'"

Readers had come to expect this kind of rich and insightful writing in the Tempo section, but for me it was a wondrous thing, even after all these years: It revealed once again the high-quality journalism that can be found in reporting that has evolved out of the kind of feature stories that once appeared in the women's and society sections.

My watch on the beat began in 1941. I was in high school, but the *Zanesville* (Ohio) *Sunday Times Signal* let me write the baby column; later I graduated to weddings and church suppers and more of the same at the *Zanesville News* during World War II. Stories expanded to include servicemen's dances and things red, white and blue.

The big break for women's sections came in the years after World War II. Returning soldiers and their sweethearts married, bought houses and had babies who demanded things. Business boomed. Advertising soared. Some lucky newspapers got so fat newsboys could hardly carry them, let alone pitch them across front lawns. Editors and writers for women's sections produced the stories to fill the added pages created by the increases in advertising. At the *Milwaukee Journal*, an editor could be notified in the morning that she had another section to edit by the end of the day.

Alas, more space did not necessarily mean better journalism. The public was getting more content, but, in the rush to fill space, the quality of stories didn't always hold up. Press releases were known to be printed verbatim, without even a courtesy of a rewrite. Big ad customers gained clout. On one city newspaper, at least, food and fashion writers received paychecks issued by the advertising department.

Perks were everywhere. Yes, there was such a thing as a free lunch, and there were freebies galore, especially cosmetics. For fashion writers, if they chose, there were paid trips to New York City to cover designer shows with information shaped and handed out by those footing the bills. *Washington Post* columnist Nicholas von Hoffman once complained in a speech at the University of Chicago that "advertisers have too long steered the women's pages." Advertising departments could force editors to print stories that advertisers wanted to see published.

By the early 1950s I was sitting at my hard-won reporter's desk in the newsroom of the *Columbus* (Ohio) *Dispatch* and reading the utter nonsense of its women's page—dressing for HIM and how to remove ink spots from a shirt. I got up and marched into editor George Smallsreed's office and applied for the job of women's editor. The editor stared back in shock. Then he said, "You're too good for that."

Clearly, women's pages were not held in high esteem, but I had a vision of what they could be with coverage of real issues and writing that ignited the imagination. I didn't share my thoughts with Smallsreed, for fear that I would not get the job. I got it.

At the rival newspaper down the street, a young woman fresh from Vassar College, Charlotte Curtis, was winning her spurs on the feisty *Columbus Citizen*. We competed for stories during the day and then met to discuss how we could save newspaper sections from ailing dullness and wafer-thin substance. Our orbits separated. Charlotte went off to the *New York Times*, where she eventually became associate editor; before that she reported on the rich and powerful, turning in social commentary unmatched to this day. The *Times'* Harrison Salisbury said of her: "Charlotte Curtis may well be the sharpest social critic of our times. It is a rapier that she conceals beneath the satin and velvet of her impeccable prose—it is a scalpel, and when her surgery is complete the victim may not even know he or she has undergone an operation." Charlotte was a reporter and editor of the paper's Family/Style section, and in January 1964 she wrote: "Society, which is periodically accused of having the zing of a wet tennis ball, has bounced back to life on America's most elegant sandbar. There is nothing relaxed, old-clothesy or understated about Palm Beach."

I went on to the *Milwaukee* (Wis.) *Journal* as society editor, reporting to the city editor. Stories with tension and discovery were there, but what was rewarding was the breaking of the crust in Upper Crust. Slide-rule editing, based on Old Family and wealth, governed the size of photos and stories for weddings. This changed when the daughter of a company president and the daughter of a factory worker in the same company exchanged vows in the same week. Their stories were paired equally, side by side, under one headline. The old formula was broken.

The society beat had its up side. In a time when jobs covering news, politics and sports were likely to go to men, society pages offered women who wanted to work on newspapers a place to start. As we wrote about weddings and births and debutante balls, we learned about the importance of rites and rituals in people's lives. We also met society editors, who were glorified as grande dames circulating with the publisher's inner circle but were frequently tough newshounds maintaining strong relationships with city desks until they turned in their white gloves.

The down side of society pages was their elitism and racism. I started working when I was in my teens; when I grew up and looked around, I realized that I had never covered anything on the "wrong side of the tracks" or been assigned to a black social event. Society sections were, after all, a reflection of their times, and there were different prejudices for different folks, depending on the geography of the newspaper. Ex-*Times*man John Corry wrote in his book *My Times* that there was a period when the society pages of the *New York Times* and the old *Herald Tribune* seldom recognized Catholics, and Irish Catholics not at all.

By the mid-'60s, frivolous society coverage was fading. A new breed of women's editors was on the scene at many newspapers. These women were not much impressed with the pretensions of high society. In some cases, they had been recruited from news departments where they temporarily had held jobs of men who had gone off to fight the Vietnam War. Their perspectives were different: "We aren't press agents grooming society's image," Frances Moffat of the *San Francisco Chronicle* told *Time* magazine in May 1967.

Moffat was one of a growing group of women agitating for news and stories about the facts of modern life. It had been going on since the '50s but with mixed success.

Bless those women editors who became morally outraged. They demanded separation of church and state—advertising and editorial—and they established policies on ethics. Reporters were forbidden to accept anything free offered by someone on the outside. Carol Sutton cut Today's Living fashion coverage at the *Louisville* (Ky.) *Courier-Journal* and assigned more stories of substance. To push this along, she set up a staff exchange program with the news department. She did so well that she became her paper's first woman managing editor and made the cover of *Time* magazine for her work at the *Courier-Journal*.

What concerned me as an editor by the '60s was the civil rights movement. At the *Milwaukee Sentinel*, photographer John Ahlhauser was sent into Mississippi to cover a brave Milwaukee debutante who was helping blacks register to vote. Ahlhauser had to switch his car's license plates; he had been warned that a Yankee from the north would be in grave danger.

The *Sentinel*'s women's section also had its own political writer, Toni McBride. She once got so caught up in an interview she was conducting at the airport with the president's daughter Lucy Johnson that she got on the plane with her and ended up in Washington, D.C., with hardly a penny in her pocket. Her dictated story was good enough to calm editor Harvey Schwander, and she got home. Liz Carpenter of Austin, Texas, author and former press secretary to Lady Bird Johnson, said McBride was far better professionally than a lot of the Washington pundits she knew.

There was still a division between two kinds of women's sections in the late '60s. One embraced the so-called American dream, à la Ozzie and Harriet; the other perceived its readers as part of the real world, curious about whatever made it go 'round. How else would SHE be a full partner to her husband or raise her children to know the truth?

On this subject, anthropologist Margaret Mead had noted that "the one-room shack, the cold water flat," and other such deviations from a comfortable standard of living, "are glossed over as accidents." The American dream was largely unchallenged in newspapers, and this became one of the responsibilities of the new women's sections and later general features sections.

Dozens of women editors who were widely separated by distance but loosely bound through a common cause—flight from fluff—embraced this and also adopted what I called beyond-the-housewife syndrome. Early efforts sometimes seemed strained, as if everyone was trying too hard. Yet the features fascinated both men and women.

The editors who were producing these stories were, for the most part, aware of and encouraged one another through their work. Some of them gathered annually at the University of Missouri where awards for the best were made by the J.C. Penney Lifestyle Journalism Program. One of the best, in my opinion, was Dorothy Jurney, former assistant managing editor of the *Detroit Free Press*. In the 1940s she had been city editor of the old *Washington News* but had to relinquish the job when the war ended. She was replaced by a man whose only experience had been as a copy boy. She trained him. Jurney later founded the think tank New Directions for News and now lives in the Philadelphia area.

The *Free Press* women's pages reported on the city's 6,000 prostitutes in May of 1967. It ranked them from chippies (who settle for a good meal and a night on the town), to streetwalkers (working at the beck of pimps and the call of drugs) to expensive suburban call girls (who keep Fanny Hill-style notes on their clients' bedroom peculiarities). The *Miami Herald* women's page gave readers women chronic gamblers who cheated; the *Seattle Times* introduced us to women alcoholics, and the *Charlotte Observer* to women in prison.

Thus did the women's revolution, primed and ready, roll into the '70s. New women's lifestyle sections respected women as readers and as participants in the world, even its seamier sides. Newspapers came to these views at various speeds. No one threw a switch on a certain day. In February of 1972 the executive editor of Long Island, N.Y.'s *Newsday*, David Laventhol, told *Time* magazine: "I feel that women's pages should be a thing of the past. They were frivolous, nonsubstantial and insulting to women." His paper's features section was called Part II. About the same time, the *Chicago Tribune*'s Sunday editor explained, "We decided a few years ago that women were interested in the same things as men." And, vice versa, I would add.

In 1971, I made a speech to an audience composed mostly of lifestyle editors at an international conference at the University of Chicago. It was titled "The Tea Party's Over, Take the Teacups Away." This was the period when Linda Witt, an author now living in Oakland, Calif., disclosed the underground abortion system that flourished by moving from house to house; she also wrote about breast implants for the fledgling Features and News syndicate in Chicago. Bright, readable, in-depth pieces on topics as diverse as Jesus freaks, Angela Davis, and death and dying appeared in lifestyle sections. I covered the very social ladies in New York state who ferried Vietnam draft dodgers into safe havens in Canada. Many of these women had young sons and were adamantly against the war. They expressed hope that someone would protect their sons if it were ever necessary.

Lifestyle journalism had come so far, yet such sections, whatever they were called, began to falter here and there in the mid-1970s for want of fresh voices. They got them when writers of the hippie generation suddenly appeared on newspaper doorsteps, though some looked as if they should instead be headed for a car wash. Creative news-trained men and women merged the newcomers with the old-timers. More exciting reading about the world in which readers lived was around the corner.

The *Chicago Tribune* created big waves in 1976 with Tempo. Storytelling originating from hard news became its trademark. Rogers Worthington went to Wisconsin and wrote about *The Progressive* magazine and its controversial printing of the recipe for the atomic bomb; editor Max McCrohon looked pained, but all he said was, "I wish I had known it was coming." When Tempo's Jeff Lyon and Peter Gorner, some time later, won a Pulitzer Prize for explanatory journalism by writing a series on breakthrough gene research, the response from then-editor James Squires had the attitude, But, of course.

Probably no other newspaper did more to propel lifestyle sections into their golden era of the '70s and '80s than the *Washington Post* with its Style section. Both Tom Kendrick and Shelby Coffey (now editor of the *Los Angeles Times*) mixed authentic journalism with delight. They let their writers show the human dimension of hard-news stories and used literary journalism to profile everyone from Alice Roosevelt Longworth at 90 to Mao Tse-tung. Anyone in public life and in national journalism had to read Style because it touched on subjects that touched them. And it assembled a collection of superb writers. Myra McPherson and Nick von Hoffman were stars. Myra was from Marquette, Mich., via the *Detroit Free Press* and the *New York Times*. Nick had been race relations reporter at the now-defunct *Chicago Daily News*.

And then there was Sally Quinn, the army brat with no formal journalism training but who could write like an angel, a prickly angel. In

June 1975, she described ballet star Rudolph Nureyev: "He has those high Tatar cheekbones, the slightly slanting eyes, the full cruel mouth slashed by an old scar, the taut muscular body, strong but gentle hands, tousled hair and a provocative half-mischievous, half-soulful look in his eyes. And, of course, there is his behind. He has a fabulous behind." Writers elsewhere tried to pace Quinn, idea for idea, and editors tried to copy Style's style, spark for spark. Impossible.

It's the '90s, however, and it's déjà vu. Many of the recent lifestyle sections I've seen appear without purpose. For one, newsrooms steal some of their best ideas, or maybe they are just reclaiming them. Unfortunately, features too often decorate newspaper front pages that are begging for hard news. Worse, perhaps, readers are left with little reason to roam inside. Can eroding ad bases be far behind?

Yet the situation is not totally out of hand. Lifestyle and general features editors simply need to find new parameters to guide them into the next century.

New structures in all walks of life are growing around us, and this has produced a great amount of frustration and anxiety and extraordinarily high stress levels. Lifestyle editors can sort through this for readers, and they can do the same with new media. Today, lifestyle sections include a walk-through of television programs; tomorrow, they must weave readers through all electronic media.

Meanwhile, fine storytelling need not—and must not—go by the wayside. No one realizes this better than Tim McNulty, the new editor of Tempo at the *Chicago Tribune*. The respected writer for the paper's Washington bureau and former correspondent to China promises "the best storytelling ever" about the slices of life.

The stories of tomorrow will be about men and women responsible for change and about quality-of-life issues. The best storytelling will instill values and pass along traditions that should not fall between the cracks. Editors will think globally as well as locally because their readers will.

We must not lose sight of the fact that lifestyle sections of the '60s, '70s and '80s that kept making 180-degree turns were frequently edited by women who had a passion for them. Now, more doors on newspapers are open to bright women journalists. They can aim to be editor, managing editor or foreign correspondent. It may be men like Tim McNulty who see new possibilities for lifestyle sections.

On Feb. 21, 1997, Tempo's cover story explained why rural radicals go against the grain. James Coate's lead went, "Long before there was a Big Apple or even a Big Easy, there was the Big Empty, the wild and wide open rural spaces of the continent known as America."

Stay tuned.

Koky Dishon, editorial consultant to React *magazine and the* South Bend *(Ind.)* Tribune, *was associate editor at the* Chicago Tribune *and the first woman on its masthead.*

11

Newsman Meets Batman

David Lieberman

Warner communications CEO Steve Ross granted few one-on-one interviews in 1989 after his movie, music and cable company agreed to merge with Time Inc. So, as a reporter covering the deal, I considered it a coup when he finally agreed to meet at Warner's munificent boardroom in midtown Manhattan.

Unfortunately, the interview was a bust. Ross—a shrewd and tough deal maker who came across as timid and eager to please—apologetically said his lawyers wouldn't let him talk about the progress of the merger. All he could do was repeat his reassuring message to government officials, who had to approve the deal, that he would protect the public interest: He promised not to interfere with the editorial independence of the journalists at Time's powerful newsmagazines, including *Time, Fortune, Sports Illustrated* and *People*.

That wasn't news. And to make the event doubly frustrating, journalistic conventions prevented me from writing the real story: Virtually everything else Ross said and did at the carefully stage-managed encounter made it clear that, despite his noble-sounding promises, he didn't value the goals of the business he was so eager to run.

The CEO started off by insisting that I put my tape recorder away. He then protected himself further by inviting about a half dozen aides to join us around the boardroom table, where they scribbled notes on legal pads. They had little to worry about. Ross only deviated from the script to rave about how successful Warner's new film, *Batman*, had been at the box office. Indeed, Ross thought it would be fun if I interviewed him while wearing a cap and pin with the *Batman* logo—and he seemed surprised when I kept refusing his repeated requests.

It was hard to imagine an entertainment executive like Ross, who died in 1992, cultivating an environment that would encourage aggressive reporting on important issues. Yet in the years following Time's merger with Warner, thousands of journalists had to figure out ways to thrive in companies obsessed with show biz. The deal abraded the long-standing view throughout government that a free press—and therefore the public interest—could only thrive in relatively small companies (by today's standards) with few conflicting interests. And that helped other moguls to launch megamergers that put them squarely into the news business.

Walt Disney Co. bought Capital Cities/ABC; News Corp. acquired New World; Westinghouse Electric won CBS—and Time Warner took control of Turner Broadcasting System. Powerful news organizations, such as ABC, CBS and CNN, and scores of local news operations became bit players in a line of business dominated by Hollywood studios.

Official concerns about media concentration date back at least as far as the 1920s. In the conferences that led to the 1927 Radio Act, for example, then-Secretary of Commerce Herbert Hoover warned that without government controls on station ownership, broadcasting might "come under the arbitrary power" of a small coterie. The law, succeeded by the Communications Act of 1934, gave federal regulators the authority to restrict ownership based on the "public interest, convenience or necessity."

In 1941 the Federal Communications Commission insisted that NBC spin off one of the two radio networks it owned, which became ABC. And in 1953 the agency adopted a rule that barred any company from owning more than seven AM, FM and TV stations.

Yet the companies that owned stations, networks and newspapers continued to grow and diversify into other businesses—publishing, music and program production. By the late 1960s, this trend so alarmed Michigan Sen. Philip Hart that he held extensive hearings on the interlocking ownership of media companies. He and other lawmakers feared that any company merely represented on a media firm's board would enjoy kid-glove coverage from its journalists.

Big deals were suspect in this environment. For example, in 1966 and 1967 the Justice Department and the FCC exhaustively investigated ITT's deal to buy ABC. Officials wanted to determine whether the sprawling conglomerate—then a major defense contractor with interests in electronics, life insurance, car rentals, consumer finance and book publishing—might compromise ABC News. By 1968, ITT lost interest in the near-bankrupt television network.

Later on, media companies used the public interest argument to fend off hostile raiders. McGraw-Hill blocked American Express's takeover effort in 1979. The financial services company, McGraw-Hill said, wouldn't protect free expression at its TV stations, books and business publications.

CBS said much the same thing in 1985 when Ted Turner tried to buy the network. The network held that Turner didn't share its passion for high-quality news. "60 Minutes" correspondent Mike Wallace dismissed the founder of CNN—then allied with conservative Sen. Jesse Helms—as an "interloper." CBS founder William Paley warned that Turner would "trifle recklessly with the company's future and the public interest." Comments like these aroused lawmakers. This possibility of government objections, plus CBS's assumption of about $1 billion in debt, prevented Turner from realizing his dream to own the Tiffany network.

But throughout the go-go years of the late 1980s, corporate raiders continued to sniff around media companies. The government had relaxed ownership restrictions on radio and TV stations, opening opportunities for big players to enjoy economies of scale. In addition, many news companies were attractive takeover targets because they had grown fat and happy. For example, *Time* magazine—part of a company long nicknamed "Paradise Publishing"—celebrated its 60th anniversary by inviting 1,700 guests to party aboard the Queen Elizabeth II. Potential acquirers saw lots of opportunities to make deals pay off simply by cutting costs.

Media executives who wanted to keep their jobs needed to show shareholders that the companies still could grow. And entertainment looked a lot more promising than news at a time when newspaper circulation and the audience for national TV news was starting to decline.

Time Inc. understood these changes as well as any company when it initiated its negotiations with Warner. Profit growth had flattened at Time's magazine division. What's more, the company's cocksure faith in its ability to invent successful publications collapsed after the 1983 fiasco with *TV-Cable Week*—a would-be competitor to *TV Guide* that was canceled after five months at a loss of $47 million.

Time's most promising businesses were its cable franchises and premium cable channel, HBO. But both were under pressure. The federal government's 1984 decision to deregulate cable kicked off a consolidation wave: Time borrowed millions to buy franchises and keep up with rivals such as Tele-Communications Inc. Meanwhile, HBO was concerned about the fast-growing competition from videocassette rentals.

Still, in 1987, Gerald Levin, then Time's strategic planner and now CEO of Time Warner, wrote in an internal memo in 1987 that "most of our asset base and expansion possibilities center on entertainment and on our established position in cable and programming. Publishing is more limited." He envisioned a merger that would turn Time into "an entertainment oriented communication company. At long last, the company would be a major motion picture producer and distributor."

It was a stunningly bold, and potentially dangerous, change in direction. The executives had to disavow the decades-old belief that big was bad, especially in the news media. Yet they had to preserve the image of themselves as uniquely qualified to appreciate and serve the public interest.

Once Time made its deal with Warner, executives argued that journalists not only wouldn't be hurt by a merger, they would be helped. A muscular Time Warner could protect the magazines' editorial freedom by fending off a hostile acquirer—possibly one from overseas—who didn't understand the need to leave reporters, editors and producers alone.

"We have never lost sight of our deep journalistic roots," the Time and Warner executives wrote in a letter to then-President Bush, "and as Time Inc. is transformed into this new venture, we pledge that the new company will remain committed to the practice of independent journalism."

This argument turned the old anti-media conglomerate logic on its head. It also enabled Time and Warner to beat back a counterproposal from Paramount Communications to pay more than $11 billion for Time. That looked like a good opportunity for Time investors, whose shares would lose value under Time's final proposal to pay $14 billion in cash and stock for Warner. To realize their merger dreams, then, Time and Warner had to convince a Delaware court to let them make the deal without a shareholder vote.

It was an unusual ploy. But the court agreed largely because Time had shown that "the mission of the firm is not seen by those involved as wholly economic." In other words, Time really did try to protect the public interest in its day-to-day work.

Big was no longer bad for journalism, and the deals that flowed from that new philosophy have profoundly influenced priorities in many major newsrooms. Entertainment conglomerates have borrowed billions to buy media companies, leaving them with insufficient resources to launch bold or extravagant ventures—especially for hard news. Time Warner, for example, seems to have given up the effort to develop conceptually new magazines. Instead, it looks for relatively risk-free opportunities to expand existing brands and franchises: *People* begot *Entertainment Weekly, Sports Illustrated* begot *SI for Kids* and a new sports news cable channel, CNN/SI.

Meanwhile, other entertainment companies have jettisoned news operations that don't mix well with show biz. Rupert Murdoch's News Corp., for example, sold most of his U.S. newspapers and magazines, including the *Boston Herald* and *New York*. And Walt Disney is now in the process of selling the newspapers it inherited, like the *Kansas City Star,* with Capital Cities/ABC.

At news operations that entertainment-oriented companies keep, ambitious journalists now see that their career ladders can reach much higher than the newsroom. They can rise farther and faster if they demonstrate that they understand entertainment and marketing as well as news.

As a result, newspeople increasingly accept the view that they can serve the public interest by producing stories that interest the public—with subjects for chitchat around the water cooler. That is most dramatically apparent in the attention paid to sensational murder cases involving O.J. Simpson, the Menendez brothers and Ennis Cosby. "True crime has established itself as a beat for mainstream journalism," says Andrew Tyndall, whose ADT Research monitors the content of the network TV newscasts. In addition, he notes that the networks spent 40 percent less time covering the 1996 presidential election than they did on the races four and eight years earlier. And coverage of international news has declined about 50 percent since the late 1980s.

Media mergers alone don't account for the recent growth of entertainment and marketing priorities in the newsroom. The public probably lost interest in foreign affairs when the Cold War ended. Washington news also became less compelling as policymakers concerned themselves more with the abstractions of deficit reduction than with galvanizing national initiatives such as highway construction, civil rights reform and putting a man on the moon.

Even before Time's deal with Warner, broadcasters had started to add music and dazzling video effects to news reports and to base stories on themes raised in movies or prime-time sitcoms and dramas. Producers had to fend off the growing competition from cable channels such as CNN and slick syndicated programs like "Entertainment Tonight." These alternatives grew after the late 1970s when satellites enabled virtually anyone to transmit instantly and inexpensively timely reports across the country. Prior to then, only the major TV networks could afford to provide live national broadcasts via AT&T's land lines.

Many journalists continued to fight the ascent of show-biz priorities up through the early 1990s. But that battle became futile in the major news organizations that were enveloped by entertainment conglomerates. Even the ones that leave newspeople free to report what they please still provide every incentive for journalists to think like marketers—obsessing about ratings and circulation.

Ross and his colleagues won the deal to merge Time and Warner. And that has made it tougher for reporters to ignore the *Batman* cap.

David Lieberman is the media business reporter for USA Today.

12

Women Sportswriters—Business as Usual

Mary Schmitt

I would have killed for one of those bathrobes. When I first started covering the NBA's Minnesota Timberwolves for the St. Paul Pioneer Press in 1989, the team provided big, plush, deep-blue bathrobes for each of the players to wear to and from the locker-room shower and, presumably, while I interviewed them.

No matter what the topic, they always looked rather debonair, lounging in front of their lockers wearing those big cushy robes, sort of like actors wearing smoking jackets. Despite what could have been an awkward situation, they always managed to look relaxed and comfortable.

In fact, as the season wore on and they got more and more used to my presence in the locker room after the game, they got more and more comfortable. So comfortable, in fact, that some players stopped wearing the robes, trading them in for towels or, in some cases, abandoning any cover-ups whatsoever.

Now this was a conundrum. In an odd way, losing the robes and towels was a signal that they had accepted my presence in the locker room. Though I certainly would have been more comfortable had they elected to continue wearing them, I was hesitant to bring this up since I would be calling attention to the fact that this was an uncomfortable situation.

What's a girl to do?

In the end, I decided not to do anything. By careful positioning and peripheral vision—not to mention that woman sportswriter's trick of carrying a really big notebook to blot out anything you don't want to see—I could tell who was and wasn't dressed, and I'd wait until a player was sufficiently clothed so that neither of us would be embarrassed during an interview.

It's a process that has served me well in my 20 years of reporting. But every woman sportswriter or broadcaster in the country—and there are more than 500 of us, including editors and public relations people—has to decide for herself how to handle the situation.

Having done that, we can get on with doing the jobs we have been hired to do. And that is a measure of how much women reporters have become a part of the sports beat, which was perhaps the last hurdle for women seeking equality in journalism.

When asked for advice on how to handle the locker-room situation—and it seems as if that is the only question people want to ask women in sports media about our jobs—I have one rule of thumb: If you act professionally, you'll be treated professionally.

In most cases. I have been lucky to avoid any controversy in my career. Oh, sure, I've been yelled at in a locker room. But it was because I was a reporter, not because I was a woman—an important distinction.

Several of my colleagues have not been as fortunate. And I'm not talking about the pioneers in my field—women like Mary Garber, Tracy Dodds, Lesley Visser, Diane K. Shah, Melanie Hauser or Betty Cuniberti—who actually stood outside locker rooms waiting for athletes to come out and talk to them after they'd finished talking to all the men reporters inside the locker room. (Don't even ask what a deadline nightmare that was. Definitely don't ask how many of the athletes confused these women reporters with fans who were waiting for autographs—or something else.)

I'm talking about women whose press credentials entitled them to be in the locker room to do their jobs. That has been standard practice in all the professional sports leagues since the mid- to late 1970s after lawsuits had been filed against professional football and baseball teams by syndicated columnist Elinor Kaine and *Sports Illustrated*'s Melissa Ludtke, respectively.

But tell that to Dave Kingman of the Oakland A's. The former player once had a rat in a box delivered to reporter Susan Fornoff in the press box.

Or tell it to the New England Patriots. Former players Zeke Mowatt, Michael Timpson and Robert Perryman were fined a total of $22,500, and the team was fined $25,000 by the NFL in November 1990 for sexually harassing sportswriter Lisa Olson of the *Boston Herald* in the locker room. For reasons unclear, the fines were never collected by the league, and the New England fans were so horrific to Olson that she fled to Australia to work.

Such instances certainly are not the norm, and they seem rather insignificant compared to many of the problems journalists face when they cover wars, civil unrest and violent crime. Every day, all across the country, women sportswriters and broadcasters—and the editors and producers in charge of them—go about their business with no problem. In fact, what most of us have found is that the battles now aren't in the field but in the office, where women in sports are facing the same kinds of glass ceilings all women in business face.

In the major professional leagues—baseball, football, basketball and hockey—all locker rooms are open to men and women after games, although the specific times they are open at other times vary from team to team. In professional golf and tennis, athletes are taken to press conferences after their competitions.

In other sports, the locker rooms are off-limits for all media. Colleges, for instance, almost always use postgame interview rooms, where fully dressed athletes meet the media—men and women.

Of course, that's not always the case. When I was in college covering the men's basketball team at Marquette University in 1975-76, and women sportswriters were still quite a novelty, coach Al McGuire didn't bat an eye when I asked to enter the locker room. In fact, he made it so easy and so much fun for an impressionable young reporter that when he was inducted into the Basketball Hall of Fame several years ago, I wrote him a note thanking him for that and telling him I wouldn't be where I was today if it hadn't been for that experience.

The fact of the matter is that by 1997, most male athletes and coaches are used to dealing with women in sports media, whether it's the reporters covering their teams or the public relations people setting up those interviews.

Do they deal with us any differently, or do we deal with them any differently than male reporters?

From my perspective, the answer, in general, is no. I might be more interested in some aspects of their lives than some other reporters— their families, for instance—and they might feel more comfortable talking to me about some things—the death of a close friend, perhaps—than with some other reporters. But I'd say that's a personal distinction, not a distinction between men and women reporters, all of whom know a good human-interest story when they see one.

Of course, I may not be the best judge. So I asked Cavaliers Coach Mike Fratello. He's been a college and professional basketball coach for almost 30 years; he also spent three years as an announcer with

NBC—and I see him every day as a sports reporter for the *Cleveland Plain Dealer*. Does he think there is a difference between the way men and women reporters approach their work?

"I think it comes down to the individual," he said. "Some men ask intelligent basketball questions because they understand the game. Other guys don't know the game and they feel like they have to ask something so they ask something. I don't think it's any different than with women. There are women who know our game and ask intelligent questions. There are others who don't. I don't think it's the sex of the reporter, it's the individual and their background of the game and the sport."

Incidentally, the gentlemanly Fratello is a fan of bathrobes, too. His players all have them. Maybe I'll get one yet.

Mary Schmitt is a sports reporter for the Cleveland Plain Dealer *who covers the Cleveland Cavaliers of the National Basketball Association.*

Part VI

The 1990s

13

Live, from the Persian Gulf War

Johanna Neuman

Bernard Shaw of CNN looked out his window at the Al Rashid Hotel in Iraq. It was the first night of the Persian Gulf War, and the allied bombing attack on Baghdad resembled firecrackers on the Fourth of July. "We see what appears to be giant sparklers," he said, "exploding balls, up in the air, one after another." It was a path-breaking report from the battlefield.

In his office at the Pentagon, Defense Secretary Dick Cheney was delighted that Americans could see and hear the war firsthand. Commentators gushed at this breakthrough marvel of technology, calling it "cable's finest hour." In the weeks to come, CNN added other distinctions to its war record. Peter Arnett stayed behind to report on the war in Iraq. Arnett was not the first reporter to drop behind "enemy lines" to report on war—Harrison Salisbury of the *New York Times* had toured North Vietnam in 1966 and reported on civilian damage from American bombs, sparking anger and loose talk in some quarters about treason. Arnett was treated to similar questions about his patriotism. This time "treason" had a television camera.

There were other moments of note. The television networks broadcast Pentagon footage of successful bombing runs and Patriot intercepts of Scud missiles, making war look to a new generation of viewers like a Nintendo game. And CNN broadcast live the briefings of American and allied military officials. This had the unintended effect of making reporters look like idiots for asking inane questions on live television. When it came time to parody the first week of the war, "Saturday Night Live" chose to satirize not the generals, or even the politicians, but the journalists. In a skit based on the daily briefings, actors playing reporters asked questions like: "Are we planning an amphibious invasion of Kuwait?"

and "Could you give us some examples of passwords that our troops use on the front lines?" and "What date are we going to start the ground attack?" It recalled that old axiom that anyone who has respect either for sausage or the law should never watch either being made. Apparently watching journalism being made was equally unattractive.

For that was the real line crossed in the Persian Gulf War, the line from packaged news to rooftop journalism. News was no longer finite, it was fluid. Writer and television critic Michael Arlen coined the term "living room war" to describe Vietnam in the 1960s. But his complaint was less about the immediacy of the coverage than about packaging of war by television executives so that it would fit between commercials. During Vietnam, film (not tape) was flown to New York for processing, arriving often days after it had been shot. There was nothing real-time about it. The news was reported, processed, filtered, edited and then finally aired on an evening news program. The new imperative in the Persian Gulf War was that footage was the fuel of a 24-hour-a-day news cycle made possible by a network of global satellites that kept information in perpetual motion. In this constant dissemination of news, no one ever said, "Goodnight, Chet." The result was a deadline every minute, no premium on checking facts and a journalism without end.

Beyond the speed of real-time information, television clung to the Doctrine of the Picture, a belief that the medium was the message. This interpretation of television's mission was not inevitable, nor healthy. In the early days of radio, Edward R. Murrow was infamous at CBS in New York for hiring reporters who could not even pass a standard voice test. He hired correspondents for their skills in the field, not in the studio. His own gift was as a narrator. Once he went out on a bombing run with a U.S. Air Force crew. After dropping bombs on Berlin "like white cookies on a black velvet night," the plane took some hits. "I mused that all men could be brave," said Murrow, "if they but left their stomachs at home."

By contrast, reporters who excelled during the Persian Gulf War were attractive (NBC's Scud Stud, Arthur Kent, was soon in demand on late-night talk shows), melodramatic (CNN's Charles Jaco liked to duck incoming Scud missiles on camera) or naive (one veteran reporter inadvertently gave Iraqis the exact position of where their Scud missiles had landed in Israel). Too often reporters were handed a microphone with little or no time to prepare and asked to broadcast.

Rooftop journalism suggested that the backdrop of a story was more important than the particulars. If Christiane Amanpour was on television, turn off the sound. This must be war. The pictures of war—not the words of a reporter—conveyed the message.

That was the Persian Gulf war's legacy for many years—that the pictures told the story, and policymakers and journalists alike were helpless in their wake. But in the six years since the end of the war, the marvel of seeing bombs fall on Baghdad, of watching history as it is made, has faded. Those pictures of Patriot missiles valiantly knocking out Scud missiles may have been fuel tanks exploding. Testimony about Iraqi troops stealing the incubators protecting Kuwaiti babies has since been called a lie. The command shelter targeted by allied "smart" bombs housed a lot of civilians. A certain public cynicism about pictures has appeared.

This is the natural order of evolution in media history. Whenever a new technology intersects with the political system, it sends shock waves through the establishment. Diplomats complain that they no longer have enough time for due deliberation, a complaint they have been making with regularity since the advent of the telegraph in the 1840s. Journalists usually boast that the new invention has given them more power and influence than ever before. "You furnish the pictures," William Randolph Hearst is said to have admonished one of his illustrators who was frustrated at a lack of action in Cuba on the eve of the Spanish-American War of 1898. "I'll furnish the war." Always, enthusiasts gush that the new technology will democratize the spread of information, and critics lament that a decentralized grip on knowledge will dilute the quality of public discourse.

The speeded flow of information inevitably changes the relationship between the audience and the policymakers. In the next war, in an age of cyberspace, real-time transmittal of information, including pictures, will be the norm. So will efforts by the Pentagon to put the best spin on the day's reports. Hopefully, access to a computerized wealth of information will prove a corrective to the rooftop journalism of the satellite generation. But enemies may take advantage of speeded data transmission to manipulate information. And political figures may find it difficult, amid the cacophony of voices and influences on the Internet, to conduct a national conversation about war and peace.

The only sure thing is that the establishment, including the mainstream media and its audience, will learn to cope. Whatever calamitous changes satellite television required, the political system has already shouldered the shock. Call it compassion fatigue or simple inoculation, satellite television has proved to be a sugar high. Once the shock wore off, the pictures lost their punch. The marvel of listening to Bernie Shaw describe the firecrackers outside his window remains, much as Edward R. Murrow's narrative remains a thrill to an earlier generation. But, happily, the hysteria about real-time news demanding instant action has calmed.

Johanna Neuman, a 1993–94 Media Studies Center fellow, is foreign editor of USA Today *and author of* Lights, Camera, War: Is Media TechnologyDriving International Politics? *(1996).*

14

A Strategy of Rape in Bosnia

Sylvia Poggioli

Rape has always accompanied war, but in the fighting that surrounded the breakup of Yugoslavia it finally received sustained attention from journalists. While years of feminist activism and scholarship have raised awareness about rape generally, in the Balkan wars the presence of women in the press corps was a vital factor in pushing rape to the top of the news. One of the reporters who covered the story was Sylvia Poggioli of National Public Radio. She spoke to Robert W. Snyder of *Media Studies Journal.*

MSJ: Rape has long been a part of war, but it seemed that in Bosnia, it got unprecedentedly extensive news coverage. By one estimate, as many as 40 percent of the press corps in Bosnia were women. Do you think that made a difference there?

SYLVIA POGGIOLI: The presence of so many women reporters in Bosnia helped destroy the myth that rape in war was a kind of business as usual. This kind of reporting showed that systematic sexual abuse of women was a central part of the specific strategy of ethnic cleansing done in the name of national and ethnic supremacy.

For centuries, rape has been treated sort of as a sideshow in wars. Usually, stories had always been done by men, for men. And women were very marginal.

In Bosnia the rapes were aimed at producing humiliation and shame and, specifically, the breakup of the family. Because that would ensure that the family would never return to its home. This was a very specific aspect of ethnic cleansing.

MSJ: Can you think of any specific incidents that you saw where women reporters took this question of rape more seriously than male reporters?

SYLVIA POGGIOLI: I can only tell you my story because it's not a subject that I have talked about that much with other women.

I came to the story a little bit later than when it first broke, which was October 1992.

When the story broke, it was really splashed all over the media. I remember a lot of newspaper reports, magazine covers with photographs of women, photographs of rape victims. When I started investigating the story, which was something like January or February of '93, I found tremendous difficulties in contacting rape victims because they'd been truly burned by the sensationalist media blitz.

Public exposure was a reliving not only of the horror of the rape but of the shame and humiliation that was experienced by the woman and her entire family. I found a lot of very intense resentment towards media intrusion because most of these women had originally been interviewed by male reporters. I even encountered several cases of women who had been hospitalized after being interviewed by foreign reporters.

So I tried to approach it from a different angle. I found a team of women psychiatrists in Zagreb who were dealing specifically with Bosnian rape victims. And they, too, encountered problems. First of all, they'd only seen a very small portion of women who had been raped—a dozen or so, who had had the courage to seek them out.

Secondly, these women were undergoing all sorts of problems as consequences of the war. They were refugees. They lost everything. They were far away from their homes. A lot of them didn't even know if their husbands were dead or alive. And some had also been abandoned by their families.

It was through these psychiatrists that I was able to contact a small number of the rape victims. But the great majority of them have really dropped out of sight. There was a kind of wall of silence around them.

MSJ: Did they ever tell you what was so bad about the interviews conducted by male reporters?

SYLVIA POGGIOLI: The intrusion. This is a patriarchal society we're talking about—all Bosnia, not just the Muslim ethnic community. And given all the horrors they had gone through—the rape, the war, everything (many of them were also pregnant)—having to relate their stories to men was certainly an extremely difficult thing. And also, I'd like to point out, at the very beginning a lot of these women were made available to the media by the Bosnian government, which also exploited this case for its own propaganda purposes.

After the government made them available, there was the personal backlash of the family. I was told by a lot of charity organizations that these women had been abandoned by their husbands and families because they couldn't deal with the stigma of the rape. So the suffering really went on and on.

I learned of cases of men who told their children: 'Don't talk to your mother. She's been sleeping with someone else.'

Now, there were religious authorities who tried to change this mindset by describing these women as heroes of the Bosnian cause because they had the courage to speak to journalists and to expose to the world what had been happening. But this had very little effect. It reminded me of what I had read about the Algerian revolution, when women who had been raped by French soldiers were also hailed by the new leaders as heroes and then immediately abandoned by their husbands.

MSJ: You worked with a translator. Did that help?

SYLVIA POGGIOLI: I did this story in Zagreb. The translator I usually worked with in Zagreb was a young man, and when we went to the hospital and talked to the psychiatrists for the first time he just panicked. He said, 'I don't think I can deal with this.'

He had worked with me for a long time—I know him well, he's a very sensitive person. I had done a lot of interviews with him of Bosnian refugees, horrible stories of ethnic cleansing in northwestern Bosnia. But he just could not deal with the rape victims.

As it turned out, the psychiatrists had a woman, an assistant who had been working with them, who spoke fluent English. And she, therefore, was the perfect person to have in that situation.

MSJ: What makes a good reporter in this kind of situation?

SYLVIA POGGIOLI: Well, I have no idea. I can tell you that this was certainly the most difficult story I've ever covered. It was emotionally draining. I don't think I'd ever spent so much time investigating a story.

I lived with it for quite a long time. It was very difficult to reach these people. And I was really worried about the danger of exploiting individual cases for sensational purposes after there had been this big media blitz.

But I really did want to show that rape was a central part of the war aim of ethnic cleansing. It was difficult. I can't tell you how to be good in these cases. It takes a lot of humility.

MSJ: Was there anything in your work that you had done before this that prepared you for this story?

SYLVIA POGGIOLI: I had interviewed a lot of refugees and certainly I had heard horrible stories. And, looking back to when I was starting to do the rape story, some of the women—the refugees I had spoken to six months earlier—had been hinting at these things.

There were very vague stories about some women disappearing in the night, but it was expressed in such terribly strange ways that you never really knew.

It's hard to probe for specific details when people are shell-shocked. I had no real training for any of this. I had always done politics or cut-and-dried stuff and, believe me, it was very hard.

In this case, certainly print reporters have an advantage. They're much more unobtrusive. Holding a microphone in front of people is very difficult.

MSJ: One woman who had made a documentary about Bosnia said that she thought that journalists often felt they pushed their professional roles to the limit, or maybe beyond the limits they had recognized previously, in trying to find some way to help people. Did you see yourself under pressure to do that?

SYLVIA POGGIOLI: Oh, many times. Many times. Whenever people heard you were from a certain country, they would, if they had relatives there, try to get you to help them—to make contact and things like this, which we always tried to do.

But it was always very difficult to get back to these people, because you never knew where they would be. You wanted very much to help them, but most of the time there was very little you could do. I didn't feel it was going over the edge of the profession at all. The problem was impotence.

MSJ: Do you think that women who report on war do it any differently, typically, from men who report on war?

SYLVIA POGGIOLI: Beyond this rape story, I don't know.

I think women may be doing fewer stories about military strategy and more stories about people. But the Bosnian war also lent itself to that because the whole purpose of the war was to attack civilians. Big strategic industries were not bombed. Factories, dams, hydroelectric power plants and things like that were not touched. The main target of the war was civilians. The idea was to move people and create as much homogeneous territory of the three communities as possible.

So the victims were always specifically the civilians, and those were the stories we told. Perhaps women had more of a tendency to do this because we—I—certainly have less interest in talking about Soviet-made tanks and *kalashnikovs*. To me, everything is a *kalashnikov*.

MSJ: Is there anything about these stories that you did and that your colleagues did back then, that hasn't held up since?

SYLVIA POGGIOLI: The overall story holds up. I think the problem is the tendency to think that there's only one bad guy.

Not enough reporting focused—or it focused too late—on what the Bosnian Croats were doing in the war between the Croats and the Muslims. There were lots of camps where the Croats held Muslims. There were rapes and atrocities on all sides. Certainly, the great, great majority were carried out by the Bosnian Serbs; they had the most weapons. They started first.

But I don't think enough was covered of the other two sides. It was always a little bit too focused on the Muslims and Serbs. I think the problem was the tendency in the Western media to think: You can't have two bad guys; it would be too complicated. It's easier just to focus on one. Very black and white, in that respect.

MSJ: Have the stories had any influence that you can discern on the war crimes trials and tribunals and investigations?

SYLVIA POGGIOLI: Certainly, I think the fact that rape was given as much coverage as it was helped. It is now being treated as a war crime at the Hague Tribunal for crimes in the former Yugoslavia. This is at

least some consolation to me for the horrors of what I saw; it served at
least that purpose.

MSJ: Could you see yourself going back, years from now, to do stories
with either the women or the children?

SYLVIA POGGIOLI: I would like to do that very much. I'm obsessed by
one woman in northwestern Bosnia. Deep down I don't believe she
could possibly be alive anymore. She was very courageous in coming
out at a very difficult time, in the middle of ethnic cleansing—she
spoke out in front of a group of militia men who then shut her up. I'm
obsessed by her; I would love to go find her, but I just can't believe that
she's alive.

MSJ: What will become of the children of some of the rapes? Could
you see yourself doing a story with one of those people, grown up,
years later?

SYLVIA POGGIOLI: Oh, yes, I could. It would be extremely difficult but
I would do it. It would be so painful. There's the chance that many of
these children could be stigmatized within their families and that, growing up with this anxiety of resentment and anger, the cycle could perpetuate itself.

MSJ: Did you learn anything covering Yugoslavia that you'd bring to
other war zones or other conflicts like it in the future?

SYLVIA POGGIOLI: I've learned how to talk to refugees. It's very difficult because it's emotionally draining. You want to say, 'Wait—where,
when, how, what happened?' And you can't. You can't. You have to let
these people give their story in their way. And so often, in the details,
they contradict themselves.

The flow of information is very difficult. But it's the problem, as a
reporter, of being intrusive in these very dramatic situations. It's tough. I
hope I don't have to do this again, very frankly. It's easier to do politics.

*Sylvia Poggioli is European correspondent for National Public Radio.
Among the awards she has received for reporting on Bosnia is a 1993
George Foster Peabody Award for a report on ethnic cleansing.*

15

Polling and "What If?" Journalism

Kathleen A. Frankovic

Polls are news. George Gallup described them as "opinion news," and opinion news deserves to be covered.

But since the 1992 California primary election, when a hypothetical exit poll result about Ross Perot was deemed more newsworthy than primary victories by George Bush and Bill Clinton, journalists have taken "opinion news" to a new level of importance. On that day journalists, claiming to offer the public the choice it "really" wanted, elevated an exit-poll result over the actual returns. They opened the door to "what if?" public opinion journalism, and that raised the risk of journalists making up the news.

Hypothetical polls are a way of asking, What if? And "what if?" journalism has always been part of election coverage. Poll questions assessing the potential impact of one candidate on another's support often tell more about a candidate's strengths and weaknesses than straightforward questions do. And putting options to the public (even extreme and impossible options) gives voters choices and helps journalists frame the debate.

In fact, "what if?" public opinion polls have a distinguished journalistic history. In 1824, when many states left the selection of their presidential electors to state legislators, not the voters, newspaper reports of polls provided the only way of measuring what voters wanted. Those poll counts (in Delaware, in Maryland and on a Mississippi riverboat, among others) frequently produced results demonstrating how out of touch state legislators were in their choice of electors.

In these 1824 "straw polls" (the name may come from the tossing of "straws in the wind"), Andrew Jackson dominated, though Henry Clay and John Quincy Adams won a few. *Niles' Weekly Register* described a

May 1824 poll meeting in Kent County, Del., as "something new...an excellent plan of obtaining the sense of the people."

The 1824 straw polls were, in many ways, even better than the real thing: the people's choice for president matters. In places where the public could vote in 1824, Jackson won more popular votes (and more electoral votes) than the other candidates. But because he didn't win a majority, the House of Representatives elected John Quincy Adams. By 1828, in part because of the straw polls' demonstration of the importance of the public's presidential preferences, nearly all the states had moved towards popular election of presidential electors.

In this century, women's organizations used hypothetical questions asked by the news media to assess the impact of nominating a women as vice president in 1984 as a tool to lobby Walter Mondale to choose New York Rep. Geraldine Ferraro. A presidential run (and perhaps a victory) by Massachusetts Sen. Ted Kennedy was polled and chronicled frequently in the 1970s.

But somehow those polls did not dominate political reporting as much as they would in 1992 and beyond. By 1992, nearly every major news organization was conducting polls, and the results reached the rest of the media through newsletters like *The Hotline*. But for reporters, they weren't substitutes for the real thing—until June 2, 1992, the last primary day of the 1992 presidential campaign season.

George Bush, the incumbent president, had clinched the Republican nomination weeks before, though Pat Buchanan kept attacking and refused to withdraw. Bill Clinton had battled back from scandals and early defeats and was on the verge of earning enough delegates to guarantee the Democratic nomination. Voters reported being dissatisfied with the campaign, and reporters were definitely bored with it. So the pollsters and journalists decided to run their own election.

The *Los Angeles Times*' exit poll asked voters in both parties: "If Ross Perot had been on the presidential ballot today, would you have voted for him?" Voter Research and Surveys, the pool of ABC, CBS, CNN and NBC, asked Democratic voters if Ross Perot had been on the Democratic primary ballot, would they have voted for former California Gov. Jerry Brown, Clinton, Perot, Paul Tsongas, Larry Agran or someone else, while Republicans got to choose among Buchanan, Bush, Perot and someone else.

According to the *L.A. Times*' poll, 51 percent of Republican voters and 45 percent of Democratic voters would have deserted their choice for Perot. The network poll found one-third of Democratic voters each supporting Perot and Clinton and the rest favoring Brown or someone else. On the Republican side, Perot would have beaten the incumbent president, 48 percent to 40 percent.

The actual returns told a different story. Voters in the California, Ohio and New Jersey presidential primaries gave Bush and Clinton clean sweeps. Clinton clinched the Democratic nomination. News organizations gave lip service to that fact, but offered other headlines and other leads about an election that never took place and whose winner wasn't even on the ballots!

Here's what the press had to say:

From the *Atlanta Constitution*: "Perot Steals Show As Clinton Goes Over the Top." From the *Chicago Tribune*: "Clinton Clinches But Perot's Shadow Looms." From the *Los Angeles Times*: "...Ross Perot...would have won both the Republican and Democratic presidential primaries in California by double-digit margins if he had been on the ballot...."

Newsday heralded the election as a "Tainted Victory," and "CBS Evening News" described "Bill Clinton's predicament."

The *Times* of London was perhaps the most blatant. It wrote "Ross Perot was the clear winner of Tuesday's California primary, even though his name was not on the ballot...."

Two days after the primary, at a journalists' forum, Hal Bruno, ABC News' director of political news, was quoted saying: "You had to be a fool not to know there was no story but Perot!"

The Perot California "victory" became part of the legacy of the 1992 campaign. References to how Perot "beat" both major parties' nominees turned up in stories about the campaign that year and beyond. And this election marked a turning point in the use of polls by media organizations.

Gallup often spoke of the glories of the pollster. "We can try out any idea...," he told me in 1983, "We can try any idea in the world!" Pollsters and journalists did their best in trying out their own ideas in 1992.

And polls highlighted the strategic issues involved in a third-party candidacy. Which party—Democratic or Republican—would be hurt more by a Perot candidacy? Later, the chairman of the Republican Party, Haley Barbour, claimed Perot voters were fundamentally Republican. Democrats argued that Perot took votes from Clinton among young people. Later, Perot himself took great notice of these hypothetical polls. He claimed that polls showed he would have won in 1992 if America had "voted its conscience." His major proposed contribution to democratic theory was his "electronic town hall," where voters could register their views by telephone or by filling out a questionnaire in *TV Guide*.

The difficulty, however, is that with so many hypothetical questions (What *if* Perot ran? What *if* his name stayed on the ballot? What *if* there were three candidates instead of two? What *if* you really had more choices? What *if* you thought Perot could win?) is that voters could make choices without consequences, and Perot could get a political free ride. In the *New Republic* of July 6, 1992, Professor Harvey Mansfield of Harvard went so far as to claim such polls "delegitimize elections" by creating candidates who exist solely because voters tell pollsters they like him more than the candidates who *are* running.

In the hypothetical polls, voters could choose multiple options without cost. Checking off a box labeled "Perot" on an exit poll didn't negate the vote just cast for Bush or Clinton. Perot always fared better in telephone surveys when a three-way alternative followed a question presenting only the major candidates as an option. When the three-way horse-race question was asked first, Perot did less well—a phenomenon that was not widely discussed. Hypothetical polls encouraged respondents to want more, and not just more choices than Bush and Clinton. Thirty-six percent wanted even more candidates than Bush, Clinton and Perot! Though two-thirds said they wanted a third party, when pressed they said it was mostly because they always preferred more choices. Journalists would report polls with great assurance, but the results were frequently due to question wording or question order, not fixed or even assured public opinion.

The 1992 California primary exit polls changed journalism. They legitimated the news value of polls examining nonexistent situations to a greater extent than ever before and attributed the characteristics of reality to findings that expressed amorphous public feelings. When the media created its own primary election in 1992, at least Ross Perot had said he would run. By the 1996 campaign, pollsters and the journalists who wrote about polls were staging an election with a candidate who never announced!

In 1995, there were 28 stories in the *Washington Post* reporting polls measuring the impact of a run by retired Gen. Colin Powell. The media pursued Powell, either in disbelief of his noncandidacy or to make a better story, and staged its own elections—even after Powell announced he would *not* run. And the media election continued even beyond the real one. On Election Day 1996, at least two networks asked "what if?" in their exit polls one more time. And it shouldn't surprise anyone that they learned that if Powell were running as an independent against Clinton and Dole, he would win.

The hypothetical polls of 1992 and 1996 often told a better story than the real elections did. The California primary exit polls spiced up campaign reporting that had gone stale, whetting journalistic appetites for more creativity in opinion coverage. Now, "what if?" public opinion journalism is a growth industry.

Kathleen A. Frankovic is director of surveys for CBS News and a spring 1997 professional-in-residence at the Annenberg School for Communication at the University of Pennsylvania.

16

Expanding the Language of Photographs

Mitchell Stephens

A photo on the front page of *New York Newsday* on Feb. 16, 1994, showed two well-known Olympic ice skaters, Tonya Harding and Nancy Kerrigan, practicing together. By the standards of the tabloid war then raging in New York City (a war *New York Newsday* would not survive), this shot of Harding and the fellow skater she had been accused of plotting to assault did not seem particularly incendiary. But there was something extraordinary about this photograph: The scene it depicted had not yet taken place. Harding and Kerrigan, as the paper admitted in the caption, had not in fact practiced together. A computer had stitched together two separate images to make it appear as if they already had.

Newsday was certainly not the first publication to have taken advantage of techniques that allow for the digital manipulation of photographs. In 1982, for example, a *National Geographic* computer had nudged two pyramids closer together so that they might more comfortably fit the magazine's cover. In July 1992, *Texas Monthly* had used a computer to place the head of then-Gov. Ann Richards on top of the body of a model riding a Harley-Davidson motorcycle. But you had to be an expert on pyramids to figure out what *National Geographic* had done, and you had to miss a fairly broad joke to take umbrage with *Texas Monthly*. *New York Newsday*'s editors had fiddled with photos featuring two of the most talked-about individuals of the day, and they weren't joking. The results of their efforts were clearly visible on newsstands all over Manhattan.

Defenders of journalism's accuracy and reliability quickly grabbed their lances and mounted their steeds: "A composite photograph is not the truth," Stephen D. Isaacs, then acting dean of the Columbia Graduate School of Journalism, thundered. "It is a lie and, therefore, a great danger to the standards and integrity of what we do." The dean of the S. I. Newhouse School of Public Communication at Syracuse University, David M. Rubin, concluded that "*New York Newsday* has taken leave of its ethical moorings."

This front-page photo in a major daily seemed to announce that craven journalists had found a powerful new way to debase themselves: computer reworkings of photographs.

Others of us, however, heard a different announcement on that winter day in 1994: *Newsday*'s rather ordinary-looking attempt to further exploit an unpleasant, mostly unimportant story, we believed, was an early indication that news images might finally be coming of age.

To understand the significance of *New York Newsday*'s digital manipulation of this photograph, it is first necessary to acknowledge all the other ways photographs are manipulated. Photographers choose angles, making sure, for example, that the crowd of reporters isn't in the shot. They use filters, adjust contrast and vary depth of field. They frame and crop, and routinely transform reds, blues and yellows into blacks, grays and whites. Aren't these distortions of sorts?

It is also necessary to acknowledge the ways in which we manipulate language. Words are routinely arranged so that they describe events that are not currently occurring, as in the sentence: "Nancy Kerrigan and Tonya Harding will practice together." Words are even deployed in tenses that describe events that likely will not or definitely will not occur: "She might have won the gold medal." And words frequently speak of one thing as if it were another: Despite its proximity to New York harbor, *New York Newsday* did not literally possess "ethical moorings." Deans Isaacs and Rubin, for all their devotion to journalistic integrity, probably did not grab lances or mount steeds. In their efforts to approach the truth, words regularly depart from the literal truth.

If fact, words have gained much of their strength through speculation, negation, hypothesizing and metaphor—through what, by Dean Isaacs's definition, might qualify as lies. In the first century and a half of their existence, photographic images, on the other hand, have been held back by their inability to speak of what will be, what might be and what won't be; their inability to present something as if it were something else. "Pictures," the theorist Sol Worth wrote dismissively in 1975, "cannot depict conditionals, counter-factuals, negatives or past future tenses." Well, now they can. Alert observers of journalism learned that on Feb. 16, 1994.

The above-board computer manipulation of photographs will give responsible journalists—those with their ethical moorings intact—a powerful new tool. Sometimes the results will be fanciful: an image of Bill Clinton and Newt Gingrich arm wrestling, perhaps. Sometimes such computer-altered photographs will be instructive: They might picture, for example, how that plane should have landed. Such reworked photos will allow us to peek, however hazily, into the future: showing not just how Harding and Kerrigan might look together on the ice but how that new building might change the neighborhood. They will also allow us to peek into the past: portraying, with photographic realism (not, as in TV reenactments, with clumsy actors), how a crime might have been committed. The idea should be to clarify, not to pretend.

For news photographs will not come of age by hoodwinking those who look at them. That must be emphasized. Before digital editing and digital photography, harried photographers occasionally rearranged backgrounds or restaged scenes; adept photo editors, armed with a thick black pencil, occasionally added hair where there was too little or subtracted a chin where there were too many. Computers make such attempts to deceive much easier but no more conscionable. There is no doubt that they have been used for such purposes—already. *Time* magazine's surreptitious digital darkening of O. J. Simpson's face on its cover later in 1994 may qualify as an example. But *New York Newsday*'s Harding-Kerrigan photo was labeled as a "composite." "Tomorrow, they'll really take to the ice together" the paper explained on that front page, though not in as large type as we journalism professors would have liked.

Here is a standard journalism deans might more reasonably champion: Digitally manipulated photographs must not be used as a tool for deceiving. They must be labeled, clearly, as what they are. (Let's take a hard line on this, initially at least: no lightening of a shadow, no blurring of an inconvenient background without some sort of acknowledgment.) But the potential these photographs offer as a tool for communicating—honestly—must not be suppressed.

With the aid of computers, photographic images will be able to show us much more than just what might present itself at any one time to a well-situated lens, as words tell us about much more than just what is, at any one time, literally the case. And computers will be able to work this magic on moving as well as still photographic images—on television news video as well as newspaper and magazine photographs.

None of this should be that hard to imagine. The computer-produced graphics that increasingly illustrate print and television news stories have been perpetrating clever and effective reimaginings of reality for many years now: politician's faces matched with piles of dollar bills, the affected states jumping out of maps, items flying in and out of shopping carts. And all this has been happening without attracting the ire of the defenders of journalism's integrity.

The notion that news photographs themselves—not just cartoon-like graphics—are subject to these new types of alteration will take some getting used to. The labels will have to be very clear, their type very large—particularly at the start. For we have been in the habit of accepting photography as what one of its inventors, William Henry Fox Talbot, called "the pencil of nature." That was always something of a misperception. Now, if we are to take advantage of the great promise of digital technology, we'll have to wise up.

For computers are going to expand our control over this pencil dramatically. Journalists will have unprecedented ability to shape the meanings their photographs, not just their sentences, can communicate. Their pictures will approach issues from many new directions. The language of photojournalism will grow. And that is good news for those who struggle to report with images.

Mitchell Stephens, a 1995–96 Media Studies Center fellow, is a professor in New York University's department of journalism and mass communications. He is author of, among other books, A History of News *(1996).*

17

The Connie Chung Phenomenon

Somini Sengupta

In 1996, the Asian American Journalists Association produced its first Men of Broadcast calendar. It was not to be a "beefcake" calendar, explained the AAJA leaders who conceived it. So there were no bare-chested guys beckoning with bedroom eyes. Instead, there was an affable Mr. March, posing with his golden retriever in front of the Golden Gate Bridge, and Mr. June, flipping burgers on a barbecue grill.

When I first came across the calendar a few months ago, it struck me as a rather poignant attempt to market Asian-American men as attractive, authoritative and, well, kind of average—all the qualities one needs to deliver the news to living rooms across America. The calendar, I was told later by former AAJA President Dinah Eng, also had a more direct mission: to show American television news directors that there were at least a dozen Asian-American men qualified to fill anchors' chairs.

And finally, Eng, a columnist and editor at Gannett News Service, explained, it was an attempt at Asian-American solidarity, "to say to our membership, 'We really care about you guys.'" (Two-thirds of AAJA's broadcast members are women.)

Even as it ostensibly sought to highlight the success of Asian-American men in broadcast, the calendar offered a stark snapshot of television journalism's Asian-American gender gap—a phenomenon that some observers have labeled "the Connie Chung phenomenon." For more than a decade, critics have noted the rise of Asian-American female reporters and anchors—even in markets with a minuscule Asian-American populace—and the relative dearth of Asian-American men. Things don't appear to have changed. Nor has the vast diversity of Asian America been represented on television: Visibly absent are Filipinos, the second largest group of Asians in the country, and South and Southeast Asians.

Industry experts will quickly tell you about the gender gap in broadcasting, period, and the difficulties of finding a male anchor (although not in the domain of network TV evening news, where, according to a study by the Center for Media and Public Affairs, in 1996 nine out of 10 network anchors were white males). Slightly more women than men are pursuing journalism degrees, and market research has debunked the old wisdom that women don't like to get their news from women. Not least of all, women sell: As some television executives have noted, the demographics most coveted by advertisers are women, 18 to 54 years old.

According to a 1995 study commissioned by the Radio and Television News Directors Fund, women occupy roughly 51.5 percent of the news anchors' seats; that doesn't include sports and weather anchors.

But throw in race and the gender gap widens. Whites are evenly split: 43 percent of all news anchors are white men, and 43 percent are white women. Among Asian-Americans, the numbers are much smaller, and the gender gap wider: 1.4 percent of all news anchors are Asian-American women, while 0.5 percent are Asian-American men. Among African Americans, the gap is sharpest: 5.5 percent of all anchors are black women and 3.2 percent are black men. Hispanic men and women occupy roughly the same share of anchors' jobs: just under 2 percent each. The same study found that 83 percent of news directors—those who hire—are men, the lion's share of them white.

Bob Papper, the Ball State University communications professor who conducted the study, cautioned that the numbers of Asian Americans are so small that they ought to be read with a grain of salt. Nevertheless, a ground-eye view seems to confirm the dearth of Asian-American men: There is James Hattori, weekend anchor at KRON-TV in San Francisco, and Fred Katayama, CNN business news anchor and correspondent. And that seems to be it.

In Asian-American circles, any discussion of why there are more women in television news is likely to fuel a prickly debate about whether and why Asian-American women are more acceptable to the largely white male news directors who hire them; the discussion then inevitably turns to the pricklier topic of why heterosexual Asian-American women disproportionately appear to date white men. We may not all be interested in that drama. But the question of this gender gap implicates all of us for the simple reason that in television the visual is vital, and an examination of who delivers our news may tell us something about whom we, as a society, have learned to trust.

To account for this gap, talent scouts and some Asian-American broadcasters offer market explanations. On the West Coast, in cities like San Francisco, where nearly a third of the populace is Asian-American, there is a handful of Asian-American men in reporting positions. But market demands don't explain the large numbers of Asian-American women on the air. Nor, noted Katayama, do they justify why a station executive once suggested innocuously that he was "needed" on the West Coast. As a third-generation Japanese American, Katayama wondered why the rest of his country should be so declared off-limits.

Some Asian-American broadcasters also offer cultural explanations. Asian parents, suggested Cindy Hsu, a daytime anchor at WCBS-TV in New York, tend not to encourage their sons to go into television journalism. With daughters, she said, they may not care as much. But then why is it, asked Ti-Hua Chang, a reporter at WNBC-TV in New York City, that many more Asian-American men appear to pursue careers in print—arguably, an even less lucrative trade than television?

And then, say men and women in broadcasting, there are the reasons unique to the peculiar institution of television news. To compete for viewers and advertisers, reporters and anchors must be viewed as authoritative, trustworthy and familiar—expectations that run counter to the dominant stereotypes of Asian men in this country.

Stereotypes, of course, are embedded in history. In the 19th century, Asian men migrated to the United States to work—under highly discriminatory conditions—building railroads, picking strawberries, mining and fishing. Under the pressure of bias and violence at the end of the 19th century, some were compelled to work as, among other jobs, laundry operators. A web of state and federal laws sharply limited their right to intermarry, to bring their families to America and to obtain American citizenship. During World War II, Korea and Vietnam, Asian men were enemy soldiers.

"Historically, as a society we have had so many conflicts with Asian countries," Eng observed, "and there's an underlying fear of seeing an Asian-American male as an authority figure."

But stereotypes can also be inconsistent: If Asian men are sometimes regarded as inscrutable and sneaky, at other times, they can be seen as spineless. On a job interview not long ago, Katayama recalled, a television executive reviewed his tapes and remarked glibly, "You know why you seem passive on the air? You can't help it. It's your culture."

"In America, people are not used to Asian men telling them things or being in positions of authority," observed Kyung Yoon, a former reporter for WNYW-TV in New York who now produces a television program for the World Bank.

But are they accustomed to Asian women in authority?

Yoon paused. "People have an easier time dealing with us," she said, because Asian-American women are seen as submissive. Many Americans may also have an easier time dealing with an Asian-American woman paired with a white male co-anchor, Yoon surmised, than a white woman paired with an Asian-American man.

Hattori, a former CBS national correspondent, chalked up the gender gap, paradoxically, to sexism against women. "I think there's still a certain acceptable exoticism that surrounds Asian women that somehow appeals to white men who are doing the watching and hiring and that doesn't apply to men in general and Asian-American men in particular."

Whatever the reasons for the on-air dearth of Asian-American men, it is clearly feeding itself. Without role models, an entire generation of Asian-American boys appears to be uninterested in a broadcast career.

"I think we start with role models," said David Louie, a business editor at KGO-TV in San Francisco and chairman emeritus of the National Academy of Television Arts and Sciences. "There also needs to be some introspection among those who hire in the industry as to whether there's a subconscious filtering process by which they automatically exclude or do not consider Asian-American males."

Still, for Asian-American women, their rise in television news has been no crystal stair. The very stereotypes that may have helped them land jobs are nevertheless damaging stereotypes that stem from images of geisha girls and war brides. And on the job, they create an uncomfortable conundrum: whether to act the part of the passive Asian woman or the hard-nosed journalist. "I found myself being more aggressive than I actually am," Yoon recalled, "just to prove I'm not that way."

Not least of all, there are the "Connie" cat-calls. "Practically every time I would go out with a camera crew, people would yell out, 'Hey, Connie Chung!'" recalled Yoon, who neither physically resembles Chung nor emulates her reporting style; Ted Koppel is more her speed.

Yoon wasn't alone in suffering the Connie comparison. In a survey conducted by Virginia Mansfield-Richardson, a Pennsylvania State University communications professor, several Asian-American women broadcasters reported being frequently referred to as Connie Chung in the field *and* in the newsroom. Many said their news directors either explicitly asked them to cultivate the Connie look or asked them to tinker with their 'dos just so, in order to approximate Chung's appearance—"a little underflip right below the ears," is how Mansfield-Richardson described it.

Connie Chung's relationship to the Asian American Journalists Association has been rocky over the years; she has only recently begun to accept the group's speaking invitations and donated money to the group. But even her critics in Asian-American circles say she has been an important pathbreaker simply by being the most prominent Asian-American face on television, one who has broken American cultural assumptions about Asian Americans. I'm yet to be convinced, though certainly she has been an important pathbreaker for Asian-American women in broadcasting.

Understandably, many Asian-American men in television are eager for breaks of their own. And that won't happen as long as news directors resist taking risks. But even if they did, it would be a mistake to assume that the simple presence of Asian-American men on television will amend coverage or advance Asian-American gender relations.

Somini Sengupta covers metropolitan news for the New York Times.

18

Covering Politics—
Is There a Female Difference?

Judy Woodruff

It was early in World War II, when many American men were heading off to fight, that 22-year-old Elizabeth Sutherland, fresh out of journalism school, made her way to Washington, D.C., from Texas to look for work as a reporter. Carrying her scrapbook of clippings around the National Press Building, she was turned down by the *New York Herald Tribune* and the *Christian Science Monitor*, among others. Elizabeth—who later became Liz Carpenter—was grateful and excited when a small agency, representing 26 daily newspapers in Michigan, hired her and gave her a pass to cover the White House. It was her "passport to the world," she recalls.

But it was a passport mostly to covering "women's angle" stories: fashion, menus and the social life of the nation's capital. There was a tiny number of women who covered politics, like Doris Fleeson of the New York *Daily News*. They were the exception. Most women reporters in the 1940s were expected to cover anything but "hard" news. (A bit of relief came from first lady Eleanor Roosevelt, who permitted only women reporters to attend her regular news conferences, where she talked of her plans to help poor women and children. In effect, she forced news outlets to hire at least one woman if they didn't already have one.)

Fast forward more than half a century to 1996, when another Texas-based reporter, Susan Feeney of the *Dallas Morning News*, found herself in the high stakes, competitive environment of a national presidential campaign. On the Bob Dole campaign plane were female reporters, TV producers, tape editors, camera operators and sound technicians. Their presence raised important points about women in the political press corps, how women report the news and the degree to which women in journalism are still disproportionately burdened by family obligations.

These women are a young, hardy and unencumbered lot. More precisely, Feeney says they took a count of themselves during one campaign trip and observed that "none had kids, but many of the guys did." She notes that many of the women with small children turn down the chance to travel on Dole's "Citizen Ship" or Air Force One and be away from home for weeks at a time. But those who do take this assignment—among them CNN's Candy Crowley, whose children are grown—say women reporters may even have an advantage: Dole, she says, "finds it hard to walk away when a woman asks him a question."

The numbers tell a story. In 1996, more than one third of the reporters covering Dole on a regular basis were women. Between 33 percent and 40 percent of the reporters covering President Clinton were female. That doesn't count all the TV and radio producers and other technical people. In all of 1972, according to Timothy Crouse's infamous *Boys on the Bus*, there were only eight women, including columnists, who appeared on the national campaign trail with any regularity. There was a distinct jump in numbers in 1984, when the candidacy of Geraldine Ferraro for vice president caused many news organizations to think about adding, or promoting, a woman reporter to the Ferraro beat. The improvement over time hasn't led to equality, but it roughly parallels the rise in the numbers of women throughout journalism since the modern women's movement got under way in the late '60s. Women today no longer hear the familiar refrain that greeted me in 1969 when, as a secretary, I asked for a reporting opportunity: "We already have a woman reporter," the news director replied.

The numbers are easy to measure; the effect is less so. At the very least, more women on the beat has caused "the boys on the bus" to clean up their act. Syndicated columnist Mary McGrory says when she joined the travelling campaign press corps in the 1960s, one male colleague, Carrol Kilpatrick of the *Washington Post*, told her how glad he was: "We were getting sloppy; we weren't shaving; we were even drinking occasionally in the morning; now that you're here, we've spruced up a lot." Further evidence came in 1984, when the Ferraro campaign attracted record numbers of women reporters, leading to a toning down of the raucous atmosphere on the campaign plane. Male reporters noted a drop in comments that might be considered sexist; more significant, men declared they had been "sensitized" by their new female reporter colleagues to Ferraro's treatment as a woman candidate.

Yet no one argues that women aren't every bit as tough in their coverage as men: from UPI's Helen Thomas to the *New York Times'* Maureen Dowd to NBC's Andrea Mitchell to CBS's Lesley Stahl, the ranks of political journalists are replete with women who have proven that they can stand up to any public official, no matter how high the rank or how intimidating the position.

On a deeper level, the debate is over whether women report the news differently. Not anymore, argues Susan Page of *USA TODAY*: she believes the sex of a reporter is no longer relevant. "The battle has been fought and won in terms of getting women into high profile political reporting jobs." CNN's Candy Crowley adds: "The bottom line is that journalists think alike; having journalism in common is a stronger bond than the differences that result from gender."

Most agree with that analysis but still see some selective issues where women provide a different perspective. NBC's Gwen Ifill says women reporters are more likely to identify with the plight of women welfare recipients and to be more interested in the subject of welfare reform. The *New York Times'* Katharine Seelye says women are more sensitive to questions about abortion, and more sympathetic to calls for family and medical leave for working parents. When Bob Dole repeatedly rejected President Clinton's advocacy of such leave in 1996, Seelye says the women reporters travelling with Dole "collectively rolled their eyes."

In California a few years ago, when then-State Treasurer Kathleen Brown revealed in a campaign debate with Gov. Pete Wilson, whom she was trying to unseat, that her daughter had been raped, *San Francisco Chronicle* political editor Susan Yoacham wrote that she was surprised and struck by how lightly Wilson seemed to take the news. Wilson later argued that Yoacham had misread his reaction, but she insists to this day that it was unnatural.

Yet, the idea of going a few steps further, and actively "pushing" a women's agenda is rejected by most female political reporters. They acknowledge that their antennae may be more attuned to some issues, but not to the point of advocacy. The year 1996 may have been the first year that women voters determined the outcome of a presidential election, but it wasn't because women reporters were pleading their case. In fact, as Feeney notes, women reporters didn't need to bring up so-called women's issues—like education, the war on drugs and family leave—because the Clinton campaign was appealing "to soccer moms every 15 minutes."

Even if it isn't seeping into their coverage, however, some issues are increasingly a part of the lives of women political reporters, particularly as their ranks grow. A prime example is the decision by more female journalists—usually mothers with small children—to turn down plum assignments on the political beat. The women covering the Dole campaign who discovered that the only parents on their plane were men—with someone staying close to home for the children—came away resigned to a different sort of inequality. As Crowley put it: "Things have changed less on the home front than on the work front."

Judy Woodruff is a prime anchor and senior correspondent for CNN. She co-anchors "Inside Politics" and "World View" daily.

19

Does the Internet Change News Reporting?
Not Quite

Elizabeth Weise

When former newsman Pierre Salinger brandished two crumpled pages at reporters on Nov. 7, 1996, and announced that he had a government document proving that the U.S. Navy accidentally shot down TWA Flight 800 while conducting missile tests off Long Island, N.Y., there were two main reactions among the media.

The mainline reporters hit the phones. They were busy calling the FBI, trying to get Salinger in Cannes, where he'd addressed his remarks to a group of airline officials, and struggling to tease out details from the document he refused to let them read.

Then there were the on-line reporters. They rushed not to the phones but to their keyboards, where they unleashed a torrent of e-mail, laughing maniacally all the while. Their fingers flew as they gasped out, "Oh my god, they think it's *real!*"

The Internet had gained another victim.

Or so it seemed. In reality Salinger was just burned by a bad source. A foreign correspondent for ABC News from 1978 to 1993, he told the AP he'd been given the document in question by "a person who got it from a person in the Secret Service" and had had it for about six weeks. He said he'd decided to take it public because the media was ignoring a report on the missile theory in *Paris-Match* the week before.

The fact that the same document had been filling up electronic mail boxes on the Net since early September just added insult to injury. Instead of a newsman making what even he admitted would "probably be the biggest mistake of my entire life," he was suddenly an old dog struck down by a new trick.

For anyone trained in the tradition of investigative journalism, where tips come from sources, from research, from having an ear to the ground, from the relentlessly posed question, where facts are to be ferreted out and pieced together, it's a brave new world indeed. The Net is a place of intrigue, rumor and fabrication. The first time you see one of the elaborate false reports or supposed trial transcripts that litter the on-line world, it seems impossible that anyone would spend so much time creating hoaxes.

But go check out any discussion group where someone has authored a 27-verse take-off on "Chattanooga Choo Choo" rewritten to feature the entire cast of *Star Wars*, or a Holocaust denier's Web site, complete with pages of footnotes or get sent a sheaf of official-sounding memos purporting to prove that Microsoft has plans to buy the Catholic Church, and suddenly the Whitewater document you've been e-mailed smells a little worse than it did before.

Salinger's problem was using an unsourced tip—it was a calculated gamble and he lost. But it wasn't the first time this has happened. A few years ago KRON-TV in San Francisco aired an amusing report about a woman who asked Neiman-Marcus for their chocolate-chip cookie recipe and was told she'd be charged "two-fifty" for it. When her bill arrived, she was appalled to find the charge was actually $250. Anchor Pete Wilson hadn't even finished reading the punch line—that the woman was now sending copies of the recipe to everyone she knew on-line to get even—when the phones started to light up with listeners eager to tell the station that they'd been caught by one of the oldest Internet gags.

But does that mean the Net is useless as a news medium? Not at all. The Internet's power lies in its immediacy, its reach and its ability to give voice to those with no access to mainstream channels of dissemination. Those who work within its weaknesses and strengths will find themselves better journalists.

Take the "hot potato" files of those investigating the Church of Scientology. In an era when even newspapers think twice about publishing anything even remotely sueable about Scientology, critics on the Net have devised elaborate schemes to pass newsletters containing detailed reports from point to point so that no one is left with incriminating evidence should Church lawyers descend with search warrants.

Or consider the *San Jose Mercury News*' 1996 series on possible CIA links to the crack cocaine trade in Los Angeles. Whether or not you believe the premise of the story, the paper's Web site made masterful use of the new medium by linking every source and reference it had to the on-line version—letting the reader, not the reporter, decide on the credibility of the claims.

And then there's the *Dallas Morning News*, which made the extraordinary decision to take its story about purported jailhouse interviews with Oklahoma City bombing suspect Timothy McVeigh straight to the Web, more than seven hours before its print edition hit the streets. In doing so, it broke the tradition that newspapers don't scoop themselves with their Web editions. And it put real-time media like radio and television on notice that newspapers are from now on a direct competitor.

And if the paper actually was trying to outrun a possible injunction by the judge because of the gag order against parties in the case, it not only succeeded, but disseminated the story so widely and made such a national splash that containment was impossible.

Each of these examples shows the depth that an instant, accessible and wildly democratic medium can bring to the practice of journalism. All that's required is a more thoroughgoing implementation of the old question "Who do you trust?" The key is remembering that while the Internet may offer enormous freedom and power, it also specializes in the anonymous, the atomized, the source without progenitor.

Every journalist makes a hundred decisions a day about the worthiness of a given source. Is the press release on university letterhead or some PR firm's? Does the invitation come from the mayor's office or a developer's?

Is the source the *Seattle Gay News* or the *New York Times*? What's the bias, who's likely to benefit, what are they leaving out?

The same set of questions in the on-line world often becomes unanswerable. The report Salinger thought he was breaking came to my e-mail box with several pages worth of headers, or return addresses. But though they traced its dissemination through numerous companies, several universities and even a government agency or two, there was no true return address, just a list of the people who'd been passing it along.

A press release comes with a phone number to call. A story in the *Economist* or the *Amsterdam News* can be traced back to a reporter, and maybe even a source. Even leaflets under car windshield wipers can be followed back to a given block, and the neighbors interviewed to find out if anyone saw who put them there.

Becoming enmeshed in the on-line world means stumbling onto lies presented as gospel truth and sprinkled with enough factoids to make them sound plausible. Because they come so crisply typed and seemingly authentically worded, the danger is that the unwary will treat them with less caution than they would a missive composed on an old typewriter and delivered in a hand-addressed envelope.

For the old guard, the task is to learn that the Internet is ultimately just one more way for information to make its way into the newsroom—and one they need to pay attention to. For the wired, it is to remember that only 23 percent of the American and Canadian public is on-line with any regularity. It's our job to sift through the blizzard of text that flows across our screens, find the real news and make sure it gets to those on the outside. Without smirking.

Elizabeth Weise is a technology writer for USA Today. *She co-edited* Wired Women: Gender and New Realities in Cyberspace *(1996). Based in San Francisco, she can be reached at <eweise@usatoday.com>.*

Part VII

Portfolio

20

Photojournalists—Visionaries Who Have Changed Our Vision

Jane M. Rosett

In the vast array of images produced by photojournalists, these stir deep emotions: Joe Rosenthal's photograph of U.S. Marines raising the American flag on Mt. Suribachi during the Battle of Iwo Jima in World War II and W. Eugene Smith's painstaking pietà image from his Minimata project of a Japanese mother bathing her suffering daughter. Although each picture works for very different reasons, together they capture divergent techniques that bring life to photojournalism.

Among photojournalists there are two types of photographers: those who lean toward the hard-news style of the Iwo Jima photo and those who lean toward the documentary style of the Minimata image. The contrast between them is the visual equivalent of hard-news writing and feature writing, of capturing an instant and exploring a story. Yet in photojournalism, as in writing, the differences between these two approaches are neither fixed nor irreconcilable.

For decades, the evolution of photojournalism has been influenced by the dialogue between documentary and hard-news photographers. From hard news comes the effort to seize the moment; from the documentary comes an immersion in the subject to create photographs that responsibly convey complex realities with great depth. Often, this immersion makes it impossible to adhere to traditional standards of objectivity.

Within this dialogue there are two tendencies that have evolved over the last 60 years. One is the rapidly shrinking distance between the subject and the lens. Photojournalism, driven by the work of pioneering photographers, has grown ever more personal, intimate and, at times, invasive. Photojournalists have also experimented with the power of still photographs to both freeze and magnify motion. In an age where journalism is surrounded by moving pictures and television, photo-journalists sought to convey movement in their picture-making techniques.

Contemporary American picture magazines trace their roots to the 1930s. The emergence of magazines such as *Life, Look, See, Photo, Picture, Focus, Pic* and *Click* provided necessary funding for protracted shooting assignments as well as publishing outlets for photojournalists' work. Equally important for the development of the documentary strain in photojournalism were the federal photographic projects of the 1930s like the Farm Security Administration, which hired photographers to document the effects of the Depression and the New Deal. Out of such work evolved ways of seeing and photographing people that enriched photojournalism.

For this founding generation of photojournalists, the influence of the 35mm range-finder camera—the precursor to the modern SLR—cannot be overemphasized. Specifically, the impact of the Leica camera's compact format, portability, ruggedness, greater depth of field and silence enabled its user to be spontaneous and mobile. Today, numerous photojournalists covet the early model M-series Leicas over more technically sophisticated equipment.

Long before the use of telephoto lenses—which enable subjects to appear closer to the lens than they actually are—Robert Capa brought us images of war that were close up and personal. He said, "If your pictures are no good, then you aren't close enough."

Capa went to the front lines of the Spanish Civil War armed with a wide-angle lens. He actually stretched the frame by getting closer to the subject, thereby recording a significantly broader image. "Falling Soldier," Capa's famous photograph of a Loyalist fighter being shot in the head outside of Córdoba, Spain, brought viewers unprecedentedly close to the realities of war. Although Capa claimed that he shot the photo on the battlefield just as machine-gun fire hit the soldier, critics have charged that, in fact, it is a carefully manipulated photo of a corpse. Regardless, Capa created an image from the front lines that has inspired generations of photographers because it reveals the precise moment of the most elusive border we know—the moment between life and death. Capa's abilities to freeze the motion of a moment and to push the boundaries of framing are still an inspiration to photojournalists.

Capa made memorable photographs for *Life*, the magazine that debuted in 1936 with a declaration—"To see life; to see the world; to eyewitness great events; to watch the faces of the poor and the gestures of the proud"—that illustrates both the idealism and arrogance of photojournalism in its infancy. That same year, Margaret Bourke-White, then known as an architectural photographer, was assigned to shoot Montana's Fort Peck Dam for *Life*'s first cover.

While in Montana, she was struck by the miserable conditions of the migrant shanty towns and photographed them. Upon Bourke-White's return, her editor, John Shaw Billings, had the innovative idea to organize a several-page layout of her photographs entitled "10,000 Montana Relief Workers Make Whoopee on Saturday Night." This spread of photographs, which expanded on a single story line, was coined the "photo essay." The practice instantly caught on and remains one of the most popular techniques for telling stories with words and pictures.

Bourke-White maintained a strict self-proscribed distance from her subjects—especially in comparison to her great contemporary, Dorothea Lange, whose photographs show a strong connection to her subjects and acknowledge their power and authority to tell their own stories. Her photographs of the Dust Bowl, which depict suffering simply and directly, convey both pain and dignity.

Lange enhanced the already-deep documentary tradition of abandoning the ruse of objectivity, the myth that photographers could somehow become involved with their subjects without forming and inserting their own points of view into the rubric of story making. *Life* magazine photographer W. Eugene Smith displayed a similarly deep, respectful and compassionate connection to the people he photographed, whether they were patients of a country doctor in Appalachia or victims of mercury poisoning in Minimata, Japan.

When photographers immerse themselves in the lives of their subjects and actually live with them, it becomes impossible to remain uninvolved. Effective documentary photography encompasses committing and engaging oneself in a collaborative picture-making process to incorporate the subject's point of view. Smith did this when he lived for three years in Minimata, documenting the devastating effects of mercury poisoning. His photographs blow away any notion of objectivity.

Smith did not shy away from the horrors he observed. He and his wife, Aileen, utilized their journalistic talents to educate the world about Chisso-Minimata disease and mercury poisoning. The Smiths were passionately committed environmentalists, and Eugene had the grace and expertise to translate his activism into his photographs, an effort that inspired the term "concerned photography." The Smiths were steadfast in their accusations of toxic environmental pollution and were well equipped with hard evidence and thorough documentation. Smith's photographs convey the tenderness he felt towards his subjects and, by extension, evoke the intensity of Smith's compassion in his readers.

Smith was an uncompromising man. In a famous fight he had with *Life* magazine editors, he dismissed two of their self-proclaimed journalistic philosophies as pure mythology: "There is no such thing as 'objective journalism' or a 'free' press." Several decades after the end of World War II, Smith dismissed his own war photographs as having been a total failure because, he argued, they had not achieved the goal of abolishing war.

In contrast to Smith's elegant style, the work of Arthur "Weegee" Fellig, a New York City ambulance chaser, blared. Amidst the cacophonous environs in which he worked, Weegee blended the hard-news photographer's instinct for breaking events, like murders, with a highly sophisticated darkroom technique.

Weegee's photography was in part distinguished by intimate glimpses of lowlifes and corpses.

His in-your-face method was widely mimicked and has since evolved into highly commercialized "paparazzi" style photography. Weegee, a civilian photographer who drove around New York City in a car equipped with a police radio, was known for beating ambulances and detectives to crime scenes. He portrayed blood and guts, corpses and mobsters, crime victims and felons—for consumption with breakfast and the morning paper. Today's television tabloid infotainment shows, which continue to sweep the Nielsen ratings, are an extension of Weegee's innovative gumption. So is the photography of Diane Arbus, who was indebted to Weegee for introducing ways to combine gritty subject matter with exquisite fine art photographic sensibilities.

As was observed by Robert Frank—a pioneer "Beat" generation artist and friend of Jack Kerouac and Allen Ginsberg who later went on to shoot editorial reportage for Black Star photo agency—the more specifically focused the work is, the more universal its message. When such specificity drew accusations that he manipulated subject matter to fit his agendas, Frank responded: "Life for a photographer cannot be a matter of indifference. Opinions often consist of a kind of criticism. Also, it is always the instantaneous reaction to oneself that produces a photograph."

News photographers are often faced with the challenge of having to translate a highly staged and visually boring event into, as Frank said, "an instantaneous reaction" that will grab readers' interest. They are further restricted by the demand for precise timing by limited shooting opportunities. A news photographer will often have a chance to shoot only a frame or two at the scene of a breaking news event. Such photography is particularly difficult when security concerns and the protocols of events create enormous physical obstacles.

Nevertheless, news photographers are expected to produce photographs of public figures that are spontaneous, one of a kind and intimate. Part of this is the result of changes in politicians' techniques of media management.

President John F. Kennedy was famous among Washington photographers for allowing unprecedented access to the first family and was quite astute at creating staged events that appeared personal. The world was allowed to see young Caroline and John-John tumbling around the White House lawn with their father looking casual with his wind-blown hair and polo shirt. While the photos from these shoots appeared to be the result of broad journalistic access granted by an easygoing, accessible administration, they were, in fact, as precisely staged as a White House press conference. This staging further advanced the expectation of the appearance of intimacy while raising the stakes for those photojournalists who, out of resentment for being manipulated by the process of these theatrical events, remained steadfastly committed to portraying reality as they saw it.

The challenge is even more difficult for photographers assigned to photograph politicians—who are posed, like actors, at a majestic and formal event—when the instruction is to make them appear accessible and warm to the viewer.

Dirck Halstead, a United Press International photographer, was assigned to cover the 1976 Democratic National Convention for Time magazine. Halstead evaluated, studied and planned for weeks how he was going to make an "intimate" photograph of the Carter-Mondale team from a cameraman's platform that was over 500 feet from the 30-foot-high podium. With the help of his editor, John Durniak, Halstead obtained a 1000mm catadioptric lens that was so heavy it took two men to carry. Halstead was restricted by available light, causing his shutter speed to be set so slow that any movement from his colleagues on the platform would kill his chance to construct the required picture. Miraculously, Halstead managed to accomplish his impossible mission: a softly focused image of an apparently spontaneous, friendly, family moment from a highly staged event.

Hard-news reporters don't usually have the luxury of Halstead's kind of preparation. More often, unique opportunities for photographs appear at random, as was the case of Eddie Adams' Pulitzer Prize-winning photo of the execution of a Viet Cong prisoner in the streets of Saigon, Feb. 1, 1968. Adams was hesitant even to pick up his camera. "I felt it was just another ordinary street arrest...." Following the lead of a Vietnamese journalist, however, Adams lifted his camera just as the prisoner was shot in the temple. This single image was perhaps the most influential to come out of the Vietnam war. It was used as ammunition both by American anti-war activists and by North Vietnamese who claimed it proved to the world that theirs was a civil war and that the United States had no business interfering.

In a marked but important contrast to the work of photojournalists who have sought to freeze motion, Sylvia Plachy's work generates motion. The streets of New York City are Plachy's beat, and, as staff photographer for the *Village Voice*, her "Unguided Tour" column intrigues readers with its informality and personal style. Plachy's photo "AIDS hearing, Queens, N.Y., 1985" is an example of how she innovatively melds her unique vision with her job as an editorial photographer out to cover a fast-breaking hard-news story. "AIDS hearing" integrates movement, not merely as a visual lure, but also as a powerful tool of rigorous reporting. Her energetic angling and peculiar point of view contribute to her editorial prowess.

Gilles Peress also incorporates motion into his photographs to emphasize his point of view. Peress dives into his work and shoots so closely that he often throws part of the frame out of focus, continuing the ever-closer relationship to the subject that has marked the evolution of photojournalism over the past six decades. His physical agility, combined with a complex political analysis, bolsters and clarifies his story line. Peress' photographs are often jarring and discomforting because he twists the action with his proximity and rolls it toward our faces with huge prints; his book *Telex Iran* is so oversized that it cannot stand upright on a shelf. While his work may be hard to look at, readers willing to commit to studying his frames will be rewarded by crisp and bold perspectives of otherwise inaccessible situations. Both Plachy and Peress share the rare talent to elevate ephemeral moments into visual masterpieces.

Photojournalism, as its hard-news and documentary styles continue to nurture each other, has brought intimacy and a sense of the surreal into everyday reportage. Photojournalists, as they refine their tools and their craft, will continue to shape the future of image-making in all visual media—not only in newspapers and magazines, but also in television and documentary film. And, as they have for decades, they will continue to create strong visual art from the fleeting moments of breaking news.

Jane M. Rosett, a photojournalist whose work has appeared in Life, Newsweek, Der Spiegel *and* Paris-Match, *has spent the past 13 years documenting the HIV/AIDS pandemic.*

Weege (Arthur Fellig) ©1994, International Center of Photography, New York, Bequest of Wilma Wilcox.
Weegee's photographs made art out of the stuff of ordinary murder stories.

Joe Rosenthal's photograph of Marines raising the flag on Iwo Jima during World War II made an instant eternal.

Eugene Smith's photograph of a mother bathing her suffering child in Minimata, Japan, evolved out of long immersion in the lives of his subjects.

Robert Capa's photograph of a soldier shot during the Spanish Civil War inspired photojournalists to get close to the action.

Margaret Bourke-White integrated images like this dance scene into photo essays that chronicled the Great Depression.

Dorothea Lange's photographs of the poor and powerless during the Great Depression were searching yet respectful.

UPI/Corbis-Bettmann

President John F. Kennedy, with his children Caroline and John, excelled at creating photo opportunities that conveyed youth and informality.

Magnum Photos

The photographs of Gilles Peress, such as this image of Iranian guards, are distinguished by innovative framing and closeness to the subject.

At the 1976 Democratic National Convention, amid thousands of people, Dirck Halstead produced an intimate photograph of the Carters and Mondales.

AP/Wide World Photos

Eddie Adams' photograph of an execution in the streets of Saigon during the 1968 Tet Offensive was, like much photojournalism, the product of a fleeting and random opportunity.

Sylvia Plachy's photograph "AIDS hearing, Queens, NY, 1985," integrates movement into a still image.

21

Editorial Cartoonists—
An Endangered Species?

Doug Marlette

"The problem with editorial cartoons," said Max Frankel, then editor of the *New York Times*, who was sitting across from me at the Pulitzer Prize luncheon at Columbia University, "is you can't edit them."

"Why would you want to?" asked my wife.

Good question. How do you edit a slam dunk? A great political cartoon is a monster jam, a scud missile, a drive-by shooting. It's also a poem, a prayer, a religious experience. It can strike at the heart like a lightning bolt from above and change the way you see and think and feel.

Who can ever forget Bill Mauldin's cartoon of the Lincoln Memorial with head bowed in hands over news of the Kennedy assassination, David Levine's Lyndon Johnson showing his appendectomy scar in the shape of a map of Vietnam, or Herblock's image of Nixon crawling out of a sewer?

When I was a boy growing up in the American South during the turbulent 1960s, I was blinded by the light of such drawings and changed forever. For a Southern Baptist Marine Corps military brat brought up in the musky recesses and brooding backwaters of the Carolina Piedmont and Black Belt Mississippi, such graven images come to you on fire, like a flaming pillar leading you out of the darkness and into the Promised Land. Bold, stark, primitive, riveting—political cartoons seemed strange and exotic like forbidden fruit, and they spoke to me in unknown tongues of peace and racial equality and social justice and the brotherhood of man. They taught me a reverence for irreverence. To this day picking up a pen or brush for me is an act of religious devotion, like handling a snake—there is something sacramental and dangerous about it, and you never know who it's going to bite.

My own personal test for greatness in cartoonists is simple. Can you remember their cartoons? It's amazing how quickly and efficiently that little test separates the sheep from the goats. We remember the cartoonists of previous decades who singed our synapses, but who's been nailing it in the '90s? Who'll be the Herblocks, Mauldins, Wrights, Conrads, MacNellys and Peters of the 21st century? Lately editorial cartoons seem to have lost their fizz. They're less substantive, less passionate, less like a surgical strike and more like a topical anesthetic that deadens us to the pain of thinking and puts us to sleep.

What happened?

To begin with, bad times for the Republic are great times for satire. Professionally, I feel lucky to have come of age at the time and place I did. Personally, the '60s were a painful time for me—my father in Vietnam, my mother falling apart emotionally at home—and a tortured time for our nation. But they were a splendid time to learn my trade. Political cartoons are custom-made for such times of tumult when everyone was wearing their hearts and brains on their sleeves, and a good cartoon was as bracing as a whiff of tear gas. At the time I thought I was smack-dab in the middle of nowhere, on the margins of the universe, stuck in Snuffdip, North Carolina, and Bass Ackwards, Mississippi. But there on the red clay piney woods battlefields of the civil rights movement, with a number 10 in the Vietnam draft lottery, my sensibilities were being forged in the fires of the moral and political questions facing America. And with a grandmother bayoneted by a national guardsman in a mill strike during the '30s, I couldn't have asked for a better pedigree to become a professional troublemaker. It was nearly impossible at the time not to have a political viewpoint. Politics, then, was not an abstraction. Politics tore us apart, divided families and split our guts over the supper table at night. Political cartoons felt to me like the most natural, visceral response to the madness of those times available to me, as natural as going to jail or burning a draft card or sitting in at a lunch counter.

I'll never forget being handed a leaflet at an anti-war demonstration emblazoned with a Don Wright cartoon showing a ghostly battalion of Vietnam casualties pointing accusatory fingers at a guilty Nixon with the caption "The Silent Majority." Here was an artist's cry of protest, his dazzling insight passed along hand to hand, like the mimeographed underground scribbles of the French Resistance or the Soviet *samizdat*. I was hooked. That's what I wanted to do.

At age 19, I drove to Washington, D.C., from Tallahassee, Fla. along with other student protesters in a broken-down Volkswagen van painted

*"Fresh, spirited American troops, flushed with victory, are bring-
ing in thousands of hungry, ragged, battle-weary prisoners . . ."*
(*News item*)

camouflage green to demonstrate in the moratorium against the Vietnam war. Somehow, between marching by candlelight to Arlington cemetery and catching my first whiff of tear gas at Dupont Circle, I called
Herblock, introduced myself as the cartoonist for the Florida State

11/7/69   THE SILENT MAJORITY

University *Florida Flambeau*, and asked to visit him at the *Washington Post*. Meeting Herblock was like meeting the North Star. He was and still is a fixed point by which we all, cartoonists and civilians alike, set our bearings. I entered his legendary cluttered office and saw his sketches for the next day's cartoon about Nixon's reaction to our peace march. Herb signed a copy of that day's drawing, looked at my cartoons and told me, as I recall, that I had a decent line and to keep plugging. All the way back to Tallahassee I had a Herblock contact high. We may not have stopped the war that day, but I had met the greatest cartoonist of the century, and I was convinced that sooner or later he would stop the war. And sure enough he did. Today, closing in on 90, he's still firing shots across the bow of the Ship of State with the same vigor with which he went after Richard Nixon and Sen. Joe McCarthy nearly 50 years ago.

But Herblock was hardly the only influence on the best cartoonists of the last 50 years. During World War II, Bill Mauldin's Willie and Joe cartoons for *Stars and Stripes* won him a Pulitzer Prize at age 24 and a nagging sense of guilt for profiting from a war that decimated so many of his generation of young men. After the war, thrown by his new celebrity, he floundered for a while drawing cartoons for a syndicate, writing books and running unsuccessfully for Congress—until 1959,

May 7, 1954

when he took over Daniel Fitzpatrick's cartooning slot at the *St. Louis Post-Dispatch*. "Hit it if it's big" was Mauldin's motto, and he updated and humanized cartooning with an elegant, semirealistic drawing style and a wit that turned more on placing public figures in humorous real-life situations than on manipulating outdated symbols and stock clichés. His bitingly fresh commentary perfectly represented the torch being passed to a new generation of cartoonists in the early '60s, when Camelot was in flower.

If Herblock and Mauldin were the twin towers of cartooning in the mainstream press at the turn of the decade, Jules Feiffer emerged on the left at the *Village Voice* as a chronicler of social malaise and ennui. With a depth and resonance unprecedented in cartooning, Feiffer taught us that a cartoonist didn't have to apologize for having a brain, that cartoons could not only be funny but have meaning. In his *Voice* drawings, Feiffer (who was also a gifted playwright) set a new standard of eloquence and sensitivity, revealing the potential of a scruffy popular art form as upper-case Art. Feiffer raised the bar for us all. Without him there would be no Garry Trudeau, no Art Spiegelman.

David Levine, Feiffer's contemporary on New York's Upper Left Side, blazed away like Daumier from his garret at the *New York Review of Books*. Levine squeezed more juice and social commentary into a single crosshatch on one of his exquisite caricatures than could be found in volumes of Victor Hugo. The influence of these two master satirists, Levine and Feiffer, echoed far beyond the limited circulations of their home-base publications.

Meanwhile, in the straight press, while Herblock imitators proliferated, two originals stood out: Paul Conrad and Pat Oliphant. Conrad, who had absorbed the jangled drawing style of the *Des Moines* (Iowa) *Register*'s J.N. "Ding" Darling growing up in Iowa, planted his "If you draw it, they will come" confidence and sprawling Midwestern expansiveness at the *Denver Post*, where he made a name for himself before joining the *Los Angeles Times*. There his uncompromising Catholic moral compass, corn-fed Midwestern sensibility and fearless prophetic stance became as foreboding a presence in LaLa Land as the San Andreas fault. Oliphant, an Australian misanthrope, took over from Conrad at the *Denver Post* and introduced America to his peculiarly down-under style—a mix of the British cartoonist Giles and *Mad*'s Jack Davis.

Oliphant touched off a frenzy of stylistic experimentation in the late '60s, encouraging cartoonists like the *Milwaukee Journal*'s Bill Sanders, the *Louisville* (Ky.) *Courier-Journal*'s Hugh Haynie and *Newsday*'s Tom Darcy to fuse a pull-no-punches approach with a bold, contemporary look. Sanders, Haynie and Darcy taught me the importance of saying something. Wayne Stayskal, a comic gem of an artist at the *Chicago Daily News*, taught me the irresistibility of humor. But for me, Don Wright, then at the *Miami News*, put it all together. He mixed the dramatic visual flair and crayon shadings of Mauldin with the sophisticated *Mad* magazine look of Oliphant, heightened to a juiciness and an edge that were all his own. I could not get enough of his cartoons. There was something sensual and wicked about them. Oliphant

SPEAKING OF AMERICAN CULTS...

had attitude but Wright combined it with moral substance and a point of view. Unfortunately, Oliphant's dazzling artistry and admirable instinct for the jugular seemed harnessed to a sour sensibility. His cartoons often looked like they were drawn by someone who had just sucked on a lemon. Oliphant was essentially giving the world the finger, while satirists like Wright and Conrad were sending it an acerbic valentine.

By the time my generation—Jeff MacNelly, Mike Peters, Garry Trudeau, Paul Szep, Tony Auth—broke onto the scene, the rules had changed, ushering in a renaissance in graphic satire. We were the first generation raised on television. *Mad* magazine made us question authority and the world of grown-ups. And that was something we could imagine doing for a living. We also were blessed with politicians who looked like their policies—LBJ, Richard Nixon, Spiro Agnew, Henry Kissinger—all living gargoyles who personified what was wrong in civil rights, Vietnam and Watergate. Such leadership ratified our killer instinct. Journalism itself had become a cauldron of insurrection. I.F. Stone, Woodward and Bernstein, and Bob Greene at *Newsday* were retooling the investigative tradition. At magazines like Harold Hayes' *Esquire* and Willie Morris's *Harper's* and Gonzo Guerilla Hunter S. Thompson's *Rolling Stone*, the New Journalism made tidal waves; their backwash showed up in cartoons.

Meanwhile, Garry Trudeau was making the comic pages safe for democracy with *Doonesbury*. Trudeau, inspired by Feiffer's existential soliloquies, used a comic strip format for his editorial commentary. He put words into the mouths of White House officials while his characters became baby-boomer archetypes and proxies for the Woodstock generation. The comics had always played host to right-wing Cold War sentiments from *Steve Canyon* and *Little Orphan Annie*; liberal opinion had been a staple of Walt Kelly's *Pogo* and Al Capp's *Li'l Abner* for years, but there was something about Trudeau's pungent liberal bias that cut against the generational grain and got him banished from the comics and onto some newspaper editorial pages, and won for him the first Pulitzer Prize awarded a comic strip.

The spirit of anarchy and insurrection loose in the land during the '70s, which found comic expression in *National Lampoon* and "Saturday Night Live," also infected the editorial pages of American newspapers. Jeff MacNelly displayed a droll, rollicking humor, an independent streak and an uncannily graceful and detailed drawing style. He won three Pulitzers, landed on the cover of *Newsweek* and was syndicated to countless newspapers. His success also inspired multiple MacNelly clones, mostly faded carbons with none of his organic creativity. Mike Peters, another singular comic talent, also stood out by bringing his scary comic genius to political issues. Though criticized by witless rivals for bringing such outright fun to the serious business of editorial commentary, his wicked cartoons skewered targets in ways his by-the-book critics could never touch. Unfortunately, the success of MacNelly and Peters legitimized a purely go-for-the-yuks cartooning style now in vogue among lesser lights, which in less deft hands becomes as brainless and boring as so much of stand-up comedy.

As the '70s moved through the Carter malaise and gave way to the Reagan Revolution, editorial cartooning seemed to mellow, reflecting the self-satisfaction of the times. The Reagan-Bush years sanctioned the rise of yuppie greed, which found its spiritual equivalent in televangelists with their gold toilet fixtures and holy wars. The acquisitiveness of the '80s was reflected in journalism as well. Instead of looking inward for inspiration, cartoonists looked more to external measures—awards, syndicate numbers and reprints, their own gold toilet fixtures—for validation and reassurance. Newsrooms brimmed with resume hounds instead of newshounds. Ambition replaced talent at drawing boards. Calculation replaced passion. Image was all. Cartoonists learned to do an impression of cartooning; they memorized the formulas and the graphic vocabulary but said nothing. Still, the '80s saw a few editorial talents emerge: Jim Borgman, with his whimsical artwork and wistful, almost shy commentary; Bill Schorr, a Peters disciple with a Disney style and a darker edge; and Tom Toles, whom editors liked for his dry wit, non-sequitur crosshatching and instruction-manual barbs garnished with enough verbiage to neuter their liberal slant—rendering them safer and somehow more civilized, like an editorial. Some of the most arresting satire of the era sprung from the comic pages with Berke Breathed's *Bloom County*. When Breathed won the Pulitzer Prize, it caused a firestorm of bitter protest from passed-over editorial cartoonists, just as it had when Breathed's comic stripper role model, Garry Trudeau, won a decade earlier.

With feminist inroads giving the green light to female aggression, editorial cartooning—like stand-up comedy—opened up to women in the '80s. Young women cartoonists M.G. Lord at *Newsday* and Signe Wilkinson at the *Philadelphia Daily News* began to make their mark, although Etta Hulme of the *Fort Worth* (Texas) *Star Telegram* had been plugging away unheralded for years. Lord, who has since abandoned cartooning and segued into a writing career, broke the glass ceiling of syndication along with Signe Wilkinson, who became the first woman cartoonist to win a Pulitzer Prize for her work. Yet the most distinctive female voices of social commentary in this period were heard not from newspaper editorial pages but from magazines. Lynda Barry and Roz Chast were the first women cartoonists to shed any visible male support or influence over their comic stylings.

Editorial cartooning in the '90s, the Clinton era, has been special so far in that nothing special has emerged. If Clinton is squishy and amorphous, so are the cartoons that mirror him. In reaction, some ink-stained ideologues are being heard from again, like Steve Benson of the *Arizona Republic* and Michael Ramirez of the Memphis, Tenn., *Commercial-Appeal*—both MacNelly clones and both blunt instruments of Republican National Committee propaganda. As in negative political

campaign ads, a certain venality has crept into cartooning, and a
clubfootedness. There's no subtlety, no discrimination, no discernment,
no selection of worthy targets. All are treated as if of equal weight, and
everyone is greeted with a sneer.

Cartoonists with a lighter touch like Steve Kelley, Chip Bok, Mike
Luckovich, Rob Rogers and Walt Handelsman are frequently reprinted,
but it's too early to tell who, if any, will be for the ages. It's easy to be
a shooting star—it's harder to have a career.

Editorial cartoonists are an endangered species. Increasingly, we're
seen as a costly indulgence. The *Greensboro* (N.C.) *Daily News* (now
the *News and Record*), a paper with an unusually rich cartooning tradition—Bill Sanders, Hugh Haynie and Bob Zschiesche got started
there—no longer has its own cartoonist. The *St. Petersburg* (Fla.) *Times*
fired one of its two cartoonists two years ago and has not rehired. The
Los Angeles Times has not replaced Paul Conrad since he went into
semiretirement three years ago.

Granted, uncertain economic times at newspapers do not embolden
editors and publishers. And in a newspaper culture increasingly obsessed with the bottom line, where a computer-generated pie chart passes
for an exciting graphic, it's no accident that I have had more cartoons
killed over the last couple of years than in the previous 25. Today,
editors think like publishers, cartoonists think like editors, and they all
think like marketing directors. They find the messy emotions that good
cartoons raise threatening, untidy, unseemly—and worse, unquanti-

HE'S GROWN A FOOT SINCE I SAW HIM LAST....

fiable. They want mush. And cartoonists whose ambition outweighs their talent or conscience are delighted to give it to them.

Has mandatory sensitivity helped geld us? Irreverence is not appreciated in an atmosphere of public piety. Interestingly, over the years I have had far more cartoons killed by liberal secular humanists than by bible-thumpers. When it comes to free speech I have found liberals more cowardly and more easily intimidated by pressure groups—perhaps because they are more guilt-driven, and easily guilt-tripped by sanctimonious special interests. If it's no longer open season for satire, if some groups are deemed exempt as fair game, if we're not all lampoonable regardless of race, creed, color, gender, whatever, then there is no free speech.

Could it be that no one needs satirists in a tabloid age when real life becomes a parody and sleaze dominates the headlines—with O.J., Michael Jackson's baby, Roseanne and the Bobbitts? Twenty-five years ago issues at the core of who we were as a nation and a people were at center stage—civil rights, Vietnam, Watergate. Now sideshows dominate, and the result is wide-scale cynicism and trivialization. Even our response to the most demented of people—John Wayne Gacy, Jeffrey Dahmer—is fascination rather than revulsion. We are too hip to be appalled, too knowing to be ashamed. That which is missing in our national ethos is missing in our editorial cartoons—passion and a sense of outrage.

Some of the most incisive editorial cartooning around today, to my eye, can be found on the pages of the *New Yorker*. Whatever the reason—perhaps due to Tina Brown ordering her cartoonists to think topical, or the ascent of Art (*Maus*) Spiegelman as art editor—the shift is noticeable and bracing. In the *New Yorker* I find what's missing in so many of today's editorial cartoons: something instinctive, unpredictable and up from the depths.

Young cartoonists seem to be struggling to find themselves, but instead of breaking new ground, creative energies are spent in rival bashing and crass self-promotion, achieving new levels of smarminess. Some cartoonists go so far as to contact newsmagazines to learn what their lead stories will be that week, the better to tailor their cartoons accordingly and increase chances for reprints. So much for fire in the belly.

If we're not an endangered species, we're certainly working hard at thinning the herd. We snipe at each other at cartoonists' conventions, whine incessantly about the successes of others and air the perennial plaint that syndication is a sellout, that the only good cartoon is a local cartoon. We spin elaborate but paper-thin self-justifications and rationalizations of our own personal failures. We make grand displays of removing ourselves from national competition, protecting our wounded

pride from further humiliation, then loudly defend our neurosis on panels and in articles, like talk-show trailer trash, making a virtue of our emotional immaturity.

Cartoonists seem especially susceptible to the kamikaze allures of self-defeat. We're constantly looking for ways to take time off, cash in our chips, remove ourselves from the game. Self-abnegation is all the rage. With comic strippers Bill Watterson, Berke Breathed and Gary Larsen deleting themselves to great fanfare, quitting is seen as a reasonable choice, even a source of pride. As we stand on the bridge to the 21st century, it's clear that as our culture devalues and co-opts the individual, the artist is neutered and the independent spirit is vanquished. So the great cartoonists may be a dying breed, either by forces beyond their control or by their own hands.

Yet the way we treat our artists, our exposed nerve endings, reveals something essential about ourselves and our nation. A great democracy needs great cartoonists because theirs is a special kind of vision.

"No eyes in your head..." we marvel with King Lear at blind Gloucester, "yet you see how this world goes."

"I see it feelingly," replies Gloucester.

Doug Marlette is a Pulitzer Prize-winning editorial cartoonist for Newsday *and an* Esquire *columnist. He is creator of the comic strip* Kudzu, *which he is adapting as a musical that will premiere in 1997 at Ford's Theater in Washington, D.C.*

Part VIII
Review Essay

22

That's the Way It Was

David T. Z. Mindich

A Reporter's Life
Walter Cronkite, Alfred A. Knopf, 1996.

11 Presidents, 4 Wars, 22 Political Conventions, 1 Moon Landing,
3 Assassinations, 2000 Weeks of News and Other Stuff on Television,
and 18 Years of Growing Up in North Carolina
David Brinkley, Ballantine Books, 1995.

A Good Life: Newspapering and Other Adventures
Ben Bradlee, Touchstone, 1995.

Volunteer Slavery: My Authentic Negro Experience
Jill Nelson, Penguin, 1993.

The Girls in the Balcony: Women, Men and The New York Times
Nan Robertson, Fawcett Columbine, 1992.

At first glance, the phrase "journalism history" may be seen as an oxymoron, like old news. Journalists, especially those on daily deadlines, must quickly record and make sense of a fiery world. Historians, on the other hand, face fewer deadlines and have the luxury of contemplation, although in stepping back from the fire, they may miss the sizzle that daily journalists enjoy. True, in the words of Phil Graham, the late publisher of the *Washington Post* and *Newsweek*, journalism is the "rough draft" of history. But the first draft and the final draft are often very different. Historians often follow the tracks of the dead, while journalists usually shine their searchlights on the living. Journalists have only days or hours or minutes to get the story right. Historians have fewer deadlines. Journalists are often forced to look at discrete events. Historians have the benefit of looking at processes that have been worked through. Truth isn't always the daughter of time, but time does make a good parent.

The journalist's memoir can be seen as an act of scooping the historians, one last attempt to make sense of a life before handing over one's notepad to others. Now, three writers, baptized by World War II, have written their memoirs. The three, Walter Cronkite, the CBS News anchor; David Brinkley, of NBC and ABC; and Ben Bradlee, the executive editor of the Washington Post during Watergate, are giants in American journalism, and their stories are significant—not only because of their authors' stature; they are so because they represent a unique historical moment, different from what came before, different from the era that replaced it.

As suggested by Brinkley's title—*11 Presidents, 4 Wars, 22 Political Conventions, 1 Moon Landing, 3 Assassinations, 2000 Weeks of News and Other Stuff on Television...*—the three journalists worked during an exciting half-century of news, having what Bradlee calls "a ringside seat at some of the century's most vital moments." Cronkite, Brinkley and Bradlee share an eagerness to cover any news, no matter how dangerous or remote, and an ability to tell a good story. Make that a great story, like the time in 1944 that Cronkite rode into combat on a glider, landing hard and taking enemy fire as he scrambled, with the others, to find his helmet. "I don't recommend gliders as a way to go to war," writes Cronkite. "If you have to go, march, swim, crawl—anything, but don't go by glider."

Or the time that David Brinkley, covering the civil rights movement for NBC, was vilified in his home state of North Carolina by an owner of a local television station. The owner called Brinkley a "nigger lover" and then went further. He found an unknown reporter, Brinkley relates, "deeply unskilled and something of a rural tinhorn" to "'answer Brinkley's lies.'" Every night this unknown reporter broadcast an excoriation of Brinkley's report. Among other things, he called the NBC correspondent a "'turncoat southerner turned northern radical.'" Brinkley, with a wit dry as talc, waits until the end of the story to tell us that his nightly accuser then parlayed his new popularity into a successful bid for the U.S. Senate as Republican Jesse Helms.

These three books are engaging and well written. Many history books are not.

The journalist acting as historian has a major advantage over the daily journalist: a perspective that is not always available in the heat of battle. When I was working for CNN in the mid-1980s, on the day that the space shuttle Challenger exploded, an excited producer told the newsroom that this would be the single most important news story of our lives. With the benefit of time, other stories—the moon landing, the assassination of the Kennedys and King, the birth of the home computer and the fall of communism, to name just a few—would prove to have greater impact. Similarly, Brinkley looks back with regret at the time he ridiculed the "Anti-Cigarette Alliance" as a bunch of weirdos. And Bradlee, who used to give a daily grade to breaking stories during Watergate, now realizes that it was foolish to give a "B+" to the revelation that Nixon had taped his conversations about the cover-up.

History, the truism goes, is written by the victors. Cronkite, Brinkley and Bradlee are victors. "Credit it all to luck, modest talent and chancing to be in the right place at the right time," wrote Brinkley. The bullets missed Cronkite as he bailed out of the glider. Brinkley joined the Army during the Second World War and was discharged for a kidney ailment he didn't have; nearly everyone in his division was killed in a freak accident in Normandy. Bradlee did not fall off the ledge he leapt onto in 1949 trying to cover a man threatening to jump.

And beyond not getting killed, the three journalists also benefited from extraordinary coincidences. Months after the Bradlees moved into their Georgetown house in 1957, the junior senator from Massachusetts moved in across the street with a child the same age as the Bradlees'. The Bradlees and Kennedys became good friends. As Kennedy's star rose, so did Bradlee's, who covered the senator for *Newsweek*.

Walter Lippmann's *Public Opinion* opens with a discussion of an island where French, English and Germans lived together in 1914. They received their news only intermittently, and for six weeks after the First World War broke out, these enemies, not knowing the reality, were friends. The anecdote serves as a metaphor for the lag between an event and the public's awareness of it.

We now live in an era in which television has significantly changed the metaphoric islands on which we live. We are connected, via cellular phones, faxes, cable and the Internet, like never before. We can watch, live, events in China.

Our age is vastly different from the earliest days of television when Brinkley and Cronkite worked. The 1952 presidential conventions were the first covered extensively by television, and the last without a keen awareness of television's reach. Brinkley recalls the NBC cameras zeroing in on a portly delegate sleeping, another dripping mustard on his tie as he ate a hot dog, and countless others reading the paper, ignoring the speeches and taking naps. Politicians had to alter their oratory: The gestures and bellowing that stirred thousands in a packed convention hall were inappropriate for reaching clusters of two or three people gathered around a television set. This new medium, television, altered public life and paved the way for presidents who understood and mastered it—Kennedy, Reagan and Clinton.

While Cronkite and Brinkley were fortunate to ride a technological upswing, the later years of their careers were marked by a new form of technology: cable television. From the time television began to reach a mass audience in the 1950s until the rise of cable and other media in the 1980s, network television was ubiquitous. During this era, when a newsman said something, it mattered, much more than it does today amid the din of so many competing voices. When Cronkite asked Sadat if he would go to Jerusalem, and then asked Begin whether Sadat would be welcome, the leaders were truly speaking to a mass audience. After Cronkite visited Vietnam and concluded, on national television, that the war was a "stalemate," Johnson threw in the towel. Brinkley, too, attracted much attention, even rising to the top of Nixon's enemy list. It's hard to imagine a journalist of today with that kind of clout.

The relationships that Cronkite, Brinkley and Bradlee had with the men who ran the country during the years after the Second World War were impressive, but in retrospect invite criticism that they could compromise the critical judgment necessary for independent journalism. Eisenhower let Cronkite and his family borrow a Scottish castle that Britain had lent him. Kennedy spent election night watching returns with Bradlee and his wife.

Postwar presidents cultivated relationships with the press that mattered, revealing and concealing information in the process. Kennedy was a master of this, as Bradlee later learned: On the one hand, Kennedy gave the *Newsweek* reporter a number of scoops; on the other hand, Bradlee did not even suspect that the president was having an affair with Bradlee's sister-in-law, Mary Pinchot Meyer. Johnson, too, shared many dinners and stories with Brinkley. On at least three separate occasions he told Brinkley about how he committed voter fraud in Texas. When first running for the Senate, Johnson and a group of friends scoured a graveyard looking for names to add to the voting rolls. When one of the friends found a stone that was difficult to read, he wanted to skip it. According to Brinkley, Johnson responded: "You will *not* skip it. He's got as much right to vote as anybody in this cemetery."

One of the greatest legacies of American journalism is its nonpartisanship and its desire and ability to play to the nation's middle. Cronkite writes that he saw his goal as a newsman to veil his opinions from his audience. "If people knew how I felt on an issue," Cronkite writes, "I had failed in my mission." Study after study has shown that contrary to the press critics of the left and right, American journalists occupy the middle of the political spectrum. In one study, most hawks and doves during the Vietnam War thought Cronkite shared their views.

John Chancellor once said, "Most reporters are members of the extreme center—I am." Cronkite, Brinkley and Bradlee seem to be members of this group, too. One of the reasons why we read memoirs by such men is the possibility of getting behind their "objective" front, to learn about their politics and passions and core values. But there is nothing interesting about their politics, that is unless you're interested in extreme centrism. True, Bradlee spent a lot of time with Kennedy, but he also was friends with Goldwater. Brinkley says he's equally dissatisfied with Democrats and Republicans. And Cronkite, citing criticism from both the right and the left, announces that he must be doing something right. I don't like "group conformity," Cronkite tells us early in his book, and I don't like "conspicuous nonconformity" either. You can't get more center than that.

This is not to say that the three journalists had no beliefs. Jack Newfield, the *Village Voice* columnist, discussing the beliefs of "objective" journalists, once wrote: "They have definite lifestyles and political values, which are concealed under the rhetoric of objectivity.... Among these unspoken, but organic, values are belief in welfare capitalism, God, the West, Puritanism, the Law, the family, property, the two-party system and, perhaps most crucially, in the notion that violence is only defensible when employed by the State." This last point is reflected beautifully in a scene in Cronkite's book in which he and his teenage daughter shout at each other across the dinner table about cop killing (she was for it, he wasn't). Whether or not Cronkite, Brinkley and Bradlee subscribe to Newfield's entire package is unclear, but Newfield's point, that journalists share core values, comes through in the books, especially Cronkite's, and most especially when Cronkite discusses Vietnam.

As it turns out, the answer to the question, Was Cronkite a hawk or a dove? is, predictably, no. During the start of the war, he, like most Americans, supported the war aims. After the Tet offensive, like most Americans, he was wary of a war that had no possible clear outcome.

After his famous trip to Vietnam, he concluded on the air: "To say that we are closer to victory today is to believe, in the face of the evidence, the optimists who have been wrong in the past. To suggest we are on the edge of defeat is to yield to unreasonable pessimism. To say that we are mired in stalemate seems the only realistic, yet unsatisfactory, conclusion." These sentences belong in the extreme center's hall of fame. Johnson, after hearing these words, is said to have uttered, "If I've lost Cronkite, I've lost middle America." Johnson was almost right. Cronkite was middle America.

In his book, Cronkite includes a picture of President Reagan, Vice President Bush, members of the cabinet, and Cronkite and CBS producer Bud Benjamin standing in a semicircle. Eight men, holding drinks and laughing over a joke. "The president had cake and champagne," Cronkite writes, "and we spent possibly two hours there in a hilarious exchange of stories—most of them dirty." The photograph, taken from 1981 seems very much dated. White men standing around telling dirty jokes has simply gotten a lot rarer.

It would be grossly unfair to single out Cronkite, Brinkley and Bradlee as representatives of the older, white male order, part of a world that excluded women and blacks. In fact, all three men were sympathetic to the civil rights and women's rights movements. One of the early defining moments for Cronkite was when his father stood up against a white man beating a black boy. Bradlee pushed his paper to report more honestly on race riots in the 1940s. And all three men, and their staffs, covered the movements of the '60s and '70s with the same courage, honesty, thoroughness and intelligence that they covered everything else.

Nevertheless, Cronkite, Brinkley and Bradlee were professionally fortunate in that they were not women or black in an era in which these groups were excluded from much of journalism. Women were excluded from the National Press Club until 1955 when they were permitted to watch from the balcony. Blacks were completely shut out of the types of jobs that Cronkite, Brinkley and Bradlee were getting in the 1940s and 1950s. Brinkley got his first job covering a president, by being "tall, white, Protestant and neatly dressed," he writes.

Women and blacks, especially blacks, were not a significant part of the journalistic universe until the 1970s. Cronkite says he did not know any blacks socially until "well after World War II." More shocking is Bradlee's admission that in 1965, "I didn't know anything about blacks, or the black experience, and I was about to become involved in the leadership of the number-one newspaper in a city that was 70 percent black, and a readership that was 25 percent black."

In 1986, Bradlee hired Jill Nelson, whose book, *Volunteer Slavery: My Authentic Negro Experience*, describes her experience working for the *Washington Post* in the late '80s and early '90s. Although this book has many flaws, it is helpful in its discussion of how the mainstream press handles black issues.

Nelson was hired five years after the *Washington Post*'s worst moment—the Janet Cooke disaster. Cooke was a talented young African-American writer who would bring fame and then disgrace to the *Washington Post* with a story, called "Jimmy's World," about an 8-year-old heroin addict. The story was widely reprinted and earned Cooke and the *Post* a Pulitzer in 1981 before Cooke confessed to making up Jimmy and his world. Nelson points out that Cooke was able to perpetuate her hoax only by playing into white stereotypes of blacks, including an environment that could produce 8-year-old heroin addicts. Bradlee's lack of experience with people like "Jimmy" and his fictional family made it easier for Cooke's hoax to go undetected. Bradlee intuitively understood Nixon and what he and his men did to retain power; Bradlee knew them personally and many others like them. But, as he admits, he had little knowledge of blacks and black issues.

I may be the first person in history to argue that Cooke's story represents progress, but it does. Certainly it was a terrible hoax, a blot on journalism. And Nelson is correct that it perpetuated stereotypes about blacks. But it also represented an early acknowledgment that stories about African Americans matter. This was not always the case, as any honest police reporter will admit.

By the time Cooke joined the *Post*, mainstream journalism was making a cognitive shift, for the better, with the acknowledgment that stories about blacks matter. It takes time to learn how to report on a community that was basically ignored. We are still learning.

Nelson's book speaks to the difficulty of undoing years of neglect. Because of her anger and ad hominem attacks, it is a problematic book: She calls the *Post* a "plantation," her bosses "ignorant caucasians" and Bradlee a "short, gray, wrinkled gnome." Half buried by her anger are some revealing and intelligent discussions of being a black reporter in a mainly white newsroom.

Soon after Nelson was hired, the *Washington Post* put out the inaugural issue of its magazine with a picture of a black man on the cover. It was titled "Murder, Drugs, and the Rap Star." The article triggered a three-month demonstration by African Americans upset by the coverage. Whether the *Post* should have run the article in its magazine's first issue is a less interesting question than the larger theme running throughout Nelson's book: that Nelson and others had a completely different worldview than the editors of the *Washington Post*. Nelson takes a definition of objectivity, "of, relating to or being an object...independent of individual thought." Yet, she writes, "at the *Washington Post* and elsewhere, objectivity is defined by the owners. Since those who run the *Post* are white men, objectivity, far from being 'independent of individual thought' is dependent upon their experience."

Cronkite's old sign off, "And that's the way it is," a neat phrase for a simpler day, simply wouldn't work in today's complex world of multiple perspectives.

Hard journalism, at least until recently, was thought of by many male journalists as a masculine endeavor. Journalism requires "staying power," wrote Whitelaw Reid in 1913. "No man who cannot, like the pugilist, 'take punishment,' has any business in it." There have always been women reporters, but until recently, few have been able to hold real power. In the *New York Times* in 1972, for example, there were no women on the masthead, no women vice presidents and one woman editor in the newsroom. Many of the handful of underpaid female reporters employed at the Times worked in the family/style section and the woman's page. Unlike the proud wall that separated news and advertising in the rest of the *Times*, the woman's page was hardly journalism at all, beholden as it was to the advertising director of the *Times*. Objectivity was seen as part of the men's sphere. The struggles of the *Times* women are depicted in an important book by Nan Robertson, *The Girls in the Balcony: Women, Men and The New York Times*.

Robertson, who began her career on the woman's page, worked her way up to a reporter in the *Times'* Washington, D.C., bureau under James Reston where she experienced the separate and unequal treatment of women by men. Reston and the men ate together at male-only clubs while the women in the bureau supped separately. Once, in 1954, Reston offered a job to a leading female reporter, Mary McGrory, under the condition that she work part-time as a switchboard operator (McGrory refused). And then there was the balcony at the National Press Club, the women's sphere.

Robertson and others formed the "Women's Caucus of The New York Times" to combat the gross inequities they found. When the Times management did not move quickly on their demands, they brought a class action suit against the paper, *Boylan et al. vs. The New York Times*. In the wake of the suit, which was settled out of court, the *Times* has made a number of changes. By 1991, two women were on the masthead; today there are four. Women make up roughly half of the new hires, and they are coming in at basically the same pay.

In 1991, the *Times* ran its controversial profile of a woman who claimed that she had been raped by William Kennedy Smith. The editors initially defended the piece but then listened to many critics who objected to the "she asked for it" tone of the piece. Three hundred *Times* employees, half men and half women, organized to protest the article. Anna Quindlen wrote a scathing criticism of her paper. Finally, Max Frankel, the executive editor, published a rare "Editor's Note" of apology. The inclusion of women had changed the *Times* forever.

Do the books by these five journalists have the perspective of historians? Yes and no. Journalists, Walter Lippmann once said, operate with searchlights, describing discrete episodes. Occasionally, this holds true for these five writers, as they report on events without stopping to interpret them. It is difficult to gain perspective in the midst of change. Robertson's book, for example, while an excellent piece of historical journalism, will one day be replaced by a more comprehensive study, when we can get a proper perspective on the inclusion of women in journalism's power structure.

These books are not so much historical analysis as much as historical artifact. At one point in his book, Cronkite expresses surprise that citizens don't march on City Hall to "demand an immediate remedy" to air pollution. The idea that City Hall can quickly remedy air pollution is an impossibly innocent one, a notion buried in amber. Perhaps that is what makes the immediate postwar era so appealing in hindsight. While no one would want us to go back to the old days, they represent an antediluvian era—before the cacophony of cable and multimedia, before the rise of a global economy, and before the multiplicity of people demanding a voice made for a better but more confusing America. The age that nurtured Cronkite, Brinkley and Bradlee represents a fossilized moment of innocence, when journalists told us the way it was, and we, more often than not, believed them.

David T.Z. Mindich, a former assignment editor for CNN and longtime print journalist, is an assistant professor of journalism at St. Michael's College. He is currently finishing a history of objectivity in Amerian journalism.

For Further Reading

Arnett, Peter. *Live from the Battlefield: From Vietnam to Baghdad, 35 Years in the World's War Zones*. New York: Simon & Schuster, 1994.

Auletta, Ken. *Three Blind Mice: How the TV Networks Lost Their Way*. New York: Random House, 1991.

Bagdikian, Ben H. *Double Vision: Reflections on My Heritage, Life, and Profession*. Boston: Beacon Press, 1995.

Barnouw, Erik. *Media Marathon: A Twentieth-Century Memoir*. Durham, N.C.: Duke University Press, 1996.

Baughman, James L. *The Republic of Mass Culture: Journalism, Filmmaking, and Broadcasting in America Since 1941*. Baltimore: Johns Hopkins University Press, 1992.

Block, Herbert. *Herblock: A Cartoonist's Life*. New York: Macmillan, 1993.

Browne, Malcolm W. *Muddy Boots and Red Socks: A Reporter's Life*. New York: Times Books, 1993.

Cloud, Stanley, and Lynne Olson. *The Murrow Boys: Pioneers on the Front Lines of Broadcast Journalism*. Boston: Houghton Mifflin, 1996.

Clurman, Richard M. *To the End of Time: The Seduction and Conquest of a Media Empire*. New York: Simon & Schuster, 1992.

Folkerts, Jean. *Voices of a Nation: A History of Media in the United States*. New York: Macmillan, 1989.

Frank, Reuven. *Out of Thin Air: The Brief Wonderful Life of Network News*. New York: Simon & Schuster, 1991.

Ghiglione, Loren. *The American Journalist: A Paradox of the Press*. Washington: Library of Congress, 1990.

Goldberg, Vicki. *Margaret Bourke-White: A Biography*. New York: Harper & Row, 1986.

Graham, Katharine. *Personal History*. New York: Alfred A. Knopf, 1997.

Griffith, Thomas. *Harry and Teddy: The Turbulent Friendship of Press Lord Henry R. Luce and His Favorite Reporter, Theodore H. White*. New York: Random House, 1995.

Hallin, Daniel C. *The Uncensored War: The Media and Vietnam*. New York: Oxford University Press, 1986.

Hamill, Pete. *A Drinking Life*. Boston: Little, Brown, 1994.

Hunter-Gault, Charlayne. *In My Place*. New York: Farrar, Straus and Giroux, 1992.

Kisseloff, Jeff. *The Box: An Oral History of Television, 1920–1961*. New York: Viking, 1995.

Koppel, Ted. *Nightline: History in the Making and the Making of Television*. New York: Times Books, 1996.

Kuralt, Charles. *A Life on the Road*. New York: Ivy Books, 1990.

Lehrer, Jim. *A Bus of My Own*. New York: G. P. Putnam's Sons, 1992.

MacNeil, Robert. *Wordstruck: A Memoir*. New York: Viking, 1989.

Mayes, Stephen. *This Critical Mirror: 40 Years of World Press Photo*. New York: Thames and Hudson, 1995.

Mills, Kay. *A Place in the News: From the Women's Pages to the Front Page*. New York: Dodd, Mead, 1988.

Prochnau, William. *Once Upon a Distant War: Young War Correspondents and the Early Vietnam Battles*. New York: Times Books, 1995.

Rather, Dan. *The Camera Never Blinks Twice: The Further Adventures of a Television Journalist*. New York: William Morrow, 1994.

Reporting World War II. New York: Library of America, 1995.

Rowan, Carl Thomas. *Breaking Barriers: A Memoir*. Boston: Little, Brown, 1986.

Salazar, Ruben. *Border Correspondent: Selected Writings, 1955-1970*. Edited and with an introduction by Mario T. Garcia. Berkeley: University of California Press, 1995.

Schudson, Michael. *Watergate in American Memory: How We Remember, Forget and Reconstruct the Past*. New York: Basic Books, 1992.

Smith, Sally Bedell. *In All His Glory: The Life of William S. Paley, the Legendary Tycoon and His Brilliant Circle*. New York: Simon & Schuster, 1990.

Steinem, Gloria. *Outrageous Acts and Everyday Rebellions*. 2nd ed. New York: Henry Holt, 1995.

Stephens, Mitchell. *A History of News*. Fort Worth, Texas: Harcourt Brace, 1996.

Trotta, Liz. *Fighting for Air: In the Trenches with Television News*. New York: Simon & Schuster, 1991.

Weaver, David H., and G. Cleveland Wilhoit. *The American Journalist in the 1990s: U.S. News People at the End of an Era*. Mahwah, N.J.: Lawrence Erlbaum, 1996.

Wolseley, Roland E. *The Black Press, U.S.A.* 2nd ed. Ames: Iowa State University Press, 1990.

Zelizer, Barbie. *Covering the Body: The Kennedy Assassination, the Media, and the Shaping of Collective Memory*. Chicago: University of Chicago Press, 1992.

Index